The Gray Book

Michael Gosney
John Odam
Jim Schmal

Designing in
Black and White
on Your Computer

Ventana Press
Chapel Hill, NC

The Gray Book
Designing in Black and White on Your Computer
© Copyright 1990 by Michael Gosney

Library of Congress Cataloging-in-Publication Data
Gosney, Michael.
      The gray book; designing in black and white on your computer/by Michael Gosney, John Odam, and Jim Schmal. — 1st ed.

     p.   cm.
   ISBN 0-940087-50-2
   1. Desktop publishing. 2. Computer graphics. I. Odam, John. II. Schmal, Jim. III. Title.
Z286.D47G68 1990
686.2'2544—dc20   90-44420
                                                         CIP

Cover design: Keith Cassell, Cassell Design, Durham, NC
Book design: The Gosney Co., Inc., San Diego, CA
Design direction: John Odam
Production supervision: Jill Malena
Graphics consultant: Jack Davis, Verbum magazine, San Diego, CA
Editorial staff: Marion Laird, Jeff Qualls

First Edition, First Printing
Printed in the United States of America
Ventana Press, Inc.
P. O. Box 2468
Chapel Hill, NC 27515
919/942-0220
FAX 919/942-1140

Trademarks

Trademarked names appear throughout this book. Rather than list the names and entities that own the trademarks or insert a trademark symbol with each mention of the trade-marked name, the publisher states that it is using the names only for editorial purposes and to the benefit of the trademark owner with no intention of infringing upon that trademark.

Copyrights

Copyrights on individual artworks reproduced in this book are retained by the originators of the artworks.

Illustration Credits

Illustrations on pages 87, 91, 92 (top), 96 (top), 102, 103 and 107 by Jack Davis. Photos on pages 81, 82, 84, 98, 99 and 101 by Craig McClain. Illustrations in Chapter 6 are credited individually. All other illustrations were created by the authors.

About the Authors

Michael Gosney is the editor and publisher of *Verbum,* the leading personal computer art journal, founding editor of *Step-by-Step Electronic Design* newsletter and president of The Gosney Company, an electronic design agency in San Diego.

John Odam is the art director of *Verbum,* design director of *Step-by-Step Electronic Design* and a nationally recognized designer specializing in electronic design and illustration.

Jim Schmal is a writer and designer with several years of experience working with desktop publishing tools. He is a contributor to *Verbum, Publish, Art Product News, Step-by-Step Electronic Design* and other publications.

Acknowledgements

The authors wish to thank, first and foremost, the many artists whose works are featured herein. Thanks also to the many individuals representing software and hardware vendors and other industry concerns who have kept us up-to-date with programs and equipment. Finally, thanks to Ventana Press for inspiring the book.

Contents

Introduction

Gray Matter and Graphic Art

Although it's not considered fine art, graphic design is creative, subjective and personal. Its functions are to inform, influence, educate, persuade and entertain.

The widespread use of laser printers and easy-to-use graphics and layout software have opened up graphic arts to thousands of professionals who otherwise might not have explored its disciplines. Surely one of the most important areas of design a desktop publisher can master is working with the surprisingly versatile palette of black, white and shades of gray.

Who Needs the Gray Book?

Although four-color printing with personal computers is now possible, most of us still rely on the classic combination of black ink on white paper. Black-and-white design is not only economical and convenient to produce, it's more appropriate than color for most purposes. Laser printers have become standard equipment, as have high-resolution imagesetting systems. And most of the documents we produce with these systems are printed in black, white and shades of gray.

If you think working in monochrome poses a severe limitation, The Gray Book will open your eyes to its endless creative possibilities. You'll learn one of the most important design skills: how to work with contrast, screens and solids to create "color" in an effective, attention-getting way.

What's Inside

The main focus of *The Gray Book* is to show desktop publishers how to create interesting printed pages in black, white and the many shades of gray in between, using basic design principles and a little imagination. Chapters One and Two focus on how to put contrast and reverses to work with a variety of black-and-white designs. Chapters Three, Four and Five explore solid grays, graduated grays, 3-D designs, lighting effects and gray-level scans—and how to use these techniques to enhance your designs. Chapter Six, "The Gray Gallery," features a rich idea bank of designs, including logos and illustrations, arranged from the simplest to the most complex.

How to Use This Book

There are few hard-and-fast rules in graphic design; the suggestions offered here aren't meant to be followed blindly. In fact, nearly all the rules of graphic design can (and should!) be broken if you know the basics outlined in The Gray Book.

We recommend that you read this book all the way through the first time. After that, you'll want to use it as a reference when you need inspiration or an inventive design solution. Use the examples in *The Gray Book* as guideposts for you to experiment on your own. And we mean experiment! As Thomas Edison said, "Genius is 1 percent inspiration and 99 percent perspiration."

If the ideas presented in these pages help inspire your own new design solutions, then *The Gray Book* has achieved its purpose. Have a great time with gray!

1
Contrast

A highlight of color on the printed page draws the eye immediately. But when you're limited to black and white, you have to be resourceful in gaining and retaining your readers' attention. *Contrast*—the juxtaposition of dissimilar elements—is one of the most effective ways of doing this.

If you've ever mixed bold type with light, placed a large headline near smaller text type or put a drop shadow behind a box, you've used contrast as a design element.

Successfully applying basic contrast principles using black, white and gray takes time and practice. That's why many of the examples in this chapter show both effective and ineffective uses of contrast. The latter part of this chapter features examples using all the forms of contrast mentioned, with varying degrees of effectiveness.

(Left) Contrast is most effective where there's a good reason to call attention to one element and downplay another. Here, the larger, blocky numeral 5 in roman type contrasts with the smaller italicized elements.

The example on the opposite page shows the use of contrast in different treatments of the same nameplate. One is black type on a white background, the other is white type *reversed* out of a black background. The reversed lettering also contrasts with the black text against the white page.

NIGHTLIFE

Lorem ipsum dolor sit amet, consectetuer adipiscing elit, sed diam nonummy nibh euismod tincidunt ut laoreet dolore magna aliquam erat volutpat. Ut wisi enim ad minim veniam, quis nostrud exerci tation ullamcorper suscipit lobortis nisl ut aliquip ex ea commodo consequat. Duis te feugifacilisi. Lorem ipsum dolor sit amet, consectetuer adipiscing elit, nibh euismod. Ut wisi enim ad minim veniam, quis nostrud exerci tation ullamcorper suscipit lobortis nisl ut aliquip ex ea commodo consequat. Duis autem dolor in hendrerit in vulputate velit esse molestie

consequat, vel illum dolore eu feugiat nulla facilisis at vero eros et accumsan et iusto odio dignissim qui blandit praesent luptatum zzril delenit augue duis dolore te feugait nulla facilisi. Lorem ipsum dolor sit amet, consectetuer adipiscing elit, sed diam nonummy nibh euismod tincidunt ut laoreet dolore magna aliquam erat volutpat. Ut wisi enim ad minim veniam, quis nostrud suscipit lobortis nisl ut aliquip ex ea commodo consequat.

NIGHTLIFE

Lorem ipsum dolor sit amet, consectetuer adipiscing elit, sed diam nonummy nibh euismod tincidunt ut laoreet dolore magna aliquam erat volutpat. Ut wisi enim ad minim veniam, quis nostrud exerci tation ullamcorper suscipit lobortis nisl ut aliquip ex ea commodo consequat. Duis te feugifacilisi. Lorem ipsum dolor sit amet, consectetuer adipiscing elit, nibh euismod. Ut wisi enim ad minim veniam, quis nostrud exerci tation ullamcorper suscipit lobortis nisl ut aliquip ex ea commodo consequat. Duis autem dolor in hendrerit in vulputate velit esse molestie

consequat, vel illum dolore eu feugiat nulla facilisis at vero eros et accumsan et iusto odio dignissim qui blandit praesent luptatum zzril delenit augue duis dolore te feugait nulla facilisi. Lorem ipsum dolor sit amet, consectetuer adipiscing elit, sed diam nonummy nibh euismod tincidunt ut laoreet dolore magna aliquam erat volutpat. Ut wisi enim ad minim veniam, quis nostrud suscipit lobortis nisl ut aliquip ex ea commodo consequat.

Lorem ipsum dolor sit amet, consectetuer adipiscing elit, sed diam nonummy nibh euismod tincidunt ut laoreet dolore magna aliquam erat volutpat. Ut wisi enim ad minim veniam, quis nostrud exerci tation ullamcorper suscipit lobortis nisl ut aliquip ex ea commodo consequat. Duis autem vel eum iriure dolor in hendrerit in vulputate velit esse molestie consequat, vel illum dolore eu feugiat nulla facilisis at vero eros et accumsan et iusto odio dignissim qui blandit praesent luptatum zzril delenit augue duis dolore te feugait nulla facilisi. Lorem ipsum dolor sit amet, consectetuer adipiscing elit, sed diam nonummy nibh euismod tincidunt ut laoreet dolore magna aliquam erat volutpat. Ut wisi enim ad minim veniam, quis nostrud exerci tation ullamcorper suscipit lobortis nisl ut aliquip ex ea commodo consequat.

Duis autem vel eum iriure dolor in hendrerit in vulputate velit esse molestie consequat, vel illum dolore eu feugiat nulla facilisis at vero eros et accumsan et iusto odio dignissim qui blandit praesent luptatum zzril delenit augue duis dolore te feugait nulla facilisi. Nam liber tempor cum soluta nobis eleifend option congue nihil imperdiet doming id quod mazim placerat facer possim assum. Lorem ipsum dolor sit amet, consectetuer adipiscing elit, sed diam nonummy nibh euismod tincidunt ut laoreet dolore magna aliquam erat volutpat. Ut wisi enim ad minim veniam, quis nostrud exerci tation ullamcorper suscipit lobortis nisl ut aliquip ex ea commodo consequat. Duis autem vel eum iriure dolor in hendrerit in vulputate velit esse molestie consequat, vel illum dolore eu feugiat nulla facilisis at vero eros et accumsan et iusto odio dignissim qui blandit praesent luptatum zzril delenit augue duis dolore te feugait nulla facilisi. Lorem ipsum dolor sit amet, consectetuer adipiscing elit, sed diam nonummy nibh euismod tincidunt ut laoreet dolore magna aliquam erat volutpat.

Ut wisi enim ad minim veniam, quis nostrud exerci tation ullamcorper suscipit lobortis nisl ut aliquip ex ea commodo consequat. Duis autem vel eum iriure dolor in hendrerit in vulputate velit esse molestie consequat, vel illum dolore eu feugiat nulla facilisis at vero eros et accumsan et iusto odio dignissim qui blandit praesent luptatum zzril delenit augue duis dolore te feugait nulla facilisi. Lorem ipsum dolor sit amet, consectetuer adipiscing elit, sed diam nonummy nibh euismod tincidunt ut laoreet dolore magna aliquam erat volutpat. Ut wisi enim ad minim veniam, quis nostrud exerci tation ullamcorper suscipit lobortis nisl ut aliquip ex ea commodo consequat. Duis autem vel eum iriure dolor in hendrerit in vulputate velit esse molestie consequat, vel illum dolore eu feugiat nulla facilisis at vero eros et accumsan et iusto odio dignissim qui blandit praesent luptatum zzril delenit augue duis dolore te feugait nulla facilisi.

Lorem ipsum dolor sit amet, consectetuer adipiscing elit, sed diam nonummy nibh euismod tincidunt ut laoreet dolore magna aliquam erat volutpat. Ut wisi enim ad minim veniam, quis nostrud exerci tation ullamcorper suscipit lobortis nisl ut aliquip ex ea commodo consequat. Duis autem vel eum iriure dolor in hendrerit in vulputate velit esse molestie consequat, vel illum dolore eu feugiat nulla facilisis at vero eros et accumsan et iusto odio dignissim qui blandit praesent luptatum zzril delenit augue duis dolore te feugait nulla facilisi. Lorem ipsum dolor sit amet, consectetuer adipiscing elit, sed diam nonummy nibh euismod tincidunt ut laoreet dolore magna aliquam erat volutpat. Ut wisi enim ad minim veniam, quis nostrud exerci tation ullamcorper suscipit lobortis nisl ut aliquip ex ea commodo consequat.

Autem vel eum iriure dolor in hendrerit in vulputate velit esse molestie consequat, vel illum dolore eu feugiat nulla facilisis at vero eros et accumsan et iusto odio dignissim qui blandit praesent luptatum zzril delenit augue duis dolore te feugait nulla facilisi.

L O R E M I P S U M dolor sit amet, consectetuer adipiscing elit, sed diam nonummy nibh euismod tincidunt ut laoreet dolore magna aliquam erat volutpat. Ut wisi enim ad minim veniam, quis nostrud exerci tation ullamcorper suscipit lobortis nisl ut aliquip ex ea commodo consequat. Duis autem vel eum iriure dolor in hendrerit in vulputate velit esse molestie consequat, vel illum dolore eu feugiat nulla facilisis at vero eros et accumsan et iusto odio dignissim qui blandit praesent luptatum zzril delenit augue duis dolore te feugait nulla facilisi.

Lorem ipsum dolor sit amet, consectetuer adipiscing elit, sed diam nonummy nibh euismod tincidunt ut laoreet dolore magna aliquam erat volutpat. Ut wisi enim ad minim veniam, quis nostrud exerci tation ullamcorper suscipit lobortis nisl ut aliquip ex ea commodo consequat.

Duis autem vel eum iriure dolor in hendrerit in vulputate velit esse molestie consequat, vel illum dolore eu feugiat nulla facilisis at vero eros et accumsan et iusto odio dignissim qui blandit praesent luptatum zzril delenit augue duis dolore te feugait nulla facilisi. Lorem ipsum dolor sit amet, consectetuer adipiscing elit, sed diam nonummy nibh euismod tincidunt ut laoreet dolore magna aliquam erat volutpat. Ut wisi enim ad minim veniam, quis nostrud exerci tation ullamcorper suscipit lobortis nisl ut aliquip ex ea commodo consequat. Duis autem vel eum iriure dolor in hendrerit in vulputate velit esse molestie consequat, vel illum dolore eu feugiat nulla facilisis at vero eros et accumsan et iusto odio dignissim qui blandit praesent luptatum zzril delenit augue duis dolore te feugait nulla facilisi.

Ut wisi enim ad minim veniam, quis nostrud exerci tation ullamcorper suscipit lobortis nisl ut aliquip ex ea commodo consequat. Duis autem vel eum iriure dolor in hendrerit in vulputate velit esse molestie consequat, vel illum dolore eu feugiat nulla facilisis at vero eros et accumsan et iusto odio dignissim qui blandit praesent luptatum zzril delenit augue duis dolore te feugait nulla facilisi.

Lorem ipsum dolor sit amet, consectetuer adipiscing elit, sed diam nonummy nibh euismod tincidunt ut laoreet dolore magna aliquam erat volutpat. *Ut wisi enim ad minim veniam, quis nostrud exerci tation ullamcorper suscipit lobortis nisl ut aliquip ex ea commodo consequat.* Duis autem vel eum iriure dolor in hendrerit in vulputate velit esse molestie consequat, vel illum dolore eu feugiat nulla facilisis at vero eros et accumsan et iusto odio dignissim qui blandit praesent luptatum zzril delenit augue duis dolore te feugait nulla facilisi.

Value Contrast

The most common sort of contrast is simply that of light and dark. When you expand your range of *value*, or *tonal*, contrast by introducing actual shades of gray into an otherwise black-and-white document, you get the benefit of yet more "color." However, it's technically possible to create a "gray" page without using any gray at all. The type on this page creates a gray shade against the white paper, which becomes more obvious if you squint at the page. The two examples above show how you can achieve varying tones of gray on a page layout using type alone. By selectively changing the face, the style (bold, italic and so on), line spacing, the case (all caps, uppercase and lowercase, small caps) or word and letter spacing, you can create a layout that is easier to read than its text-intensive counterpart.

Notice how the page on the right is more "textured," visually appealing and inviting to read than the one on the left.

Simple but boring. There are two different "colors" at work here, one for the headline and one for the body copy.

SEVENTH INNING STRETCH

Lorem ipsum dolor sit amet, consectetuer adipiscing elit, sed diam nonummy nibh euismod tincidunt ut laoreet dolore magna aliquam erat volutpat. Ut wisi enim ad minim veniam, quis nostrud exerci tation ullamcorper suscipit lobortis nisl ut aliquip ex ea commodo consequat. Duis te feugait nulla facilisi. Lorem ipsum dolor sit amet, consectetuer adipiscing elit, nibh euismod. Ut wisi enim ad minim veniam, quis nostrud exerci tation ullamcorper suscipit lobortis nisl ut aliquip ex ea commodo consequat. Duis autem vel eum iriure dolor in hendrerit in vulputate velit esse molestie consequat, vel illum dolore eu feugiat nulla facilisis at vero eros et accumsan et iusto odio dignissim qui blandit praesent luptatum zzril delenit augue duis dolore te feugait nulla facilisi. Lorem ipsum dolor sit

amet, consectetuer adipiscing elit, sed diam nonummy nibh euismod tincidunt ut laoreet dolore magna aliquam erat volutpat. Ut wisi enim ad minim veniam, quis nostrud exerci tation ullamcorper suscipit lobortis nisl ut aliquip ex ea commodo consequat. Duis autem vel iriure dolor in hendrerit in vulputate velit esse molestie consequat, vel illum dolore eu feugiat nulla facilisis at vero ero delenit augue duis dolore te feugait nulla facilisi. Consectetuer adipiscing elit, sed diam nonummy nibh euismod tincidunt ut laoreet dolore magna aliquam erat volutpat. Ut wisi enim ad minim veniam, quis nostrud exerci tation ullamcorper suscipit lobortis nisl ut aliquip ex consequat. Duis autem vel eum iriure dolor velit esse molestie consequat, vel illum dolore eu feugiat nulla odio dignissim qui blandit praesent

luptatum zzril delim ad minim veniam, quis nostrud exerci tation ullamcorper suscipit lobortis nisl ut aliquip ex ea commodo consequat. Duis te feugait nulla facilisi. Lorem ipsum dolor sit amet, consectetuer adipiscing elit, sed diam nonummy nibh euismod tincidunt ut laoreet dolore magna aliquam erat volutpat. Ut wisi enim ad minim veniam, im ad minim veniam, quis nostrud exerci tation ullamcorper suscipit lobortis nisl ut aliquip ex ea commodo consequat. Duis te feugait nulla facilisi. Lorem ipsum dolor sit amet, consectetuer adipiscing elit, sed diam nonummy nibh euismod tincidunt ut laoreet ullamcorper suscipit lobortis nisl ut aliquip ex ea commodo consequat. Duis autem vel eum iriure dolim ad minim veniam, quis nostrud exerci tation ullamcorper suscipit lobortis nisl

---

A big improvement: now there are four "colors." Note that it wasn't necessary to change the type size of the headline, just increase the letter spacing and boldface the paragraph lead-ins.

SEVENTH INNING
S T R E T C H

Consectetuer adipiscing elit, sed diam nonummy nibh euismod tincidunt ut laoreet dolore magna aliquam erat volutpat. Ut wisi enim ad minim veniam, quis nostrud exerci tation ullamcorper suscipit lobortis nisl ut aliquip ex ea commodo consequat. Duis te feugait nulla facilisi.
Lorem ipsum dolor sit amet Ut wisi enim ad minim veniam, quis nostrud exerci tation ullamcorper suscipit lobortis nisl ut aliquip ex ea commodo consequat. Duis autem vel eum iriure dolor in hendrerit in vulputate velit esse molestie consequat, vel illum dolore eu feugiat nulla facilisis at vero eros et accumsan et iusto odio dignissim qui blandit praesent luptatum zzril delenit augue duis dolore te feugait nulla facilisi. Lorem ipsum dolor sit amet, consectetuer adipiscing elit, sed diam nonummy nibh euismod

tincidunt ut laoreet dolore magna aliquam erat volutpat. Ut wisi enim ad minim veniam, quis nostrud exerci tation ullamcorper suscipit lobortis nisl ut aliquip ex ea commodo consequat. Duis autem vel iriure dolor in hendrerit in vulputate velit esse
Molestie consequat Cons ectetuer adipiscing elit, sed diam nonummy nibh euismod tincidunt ut laoreet dolore magna aliquam erat volutpat. Ut wisi enim ad minim veniam, quis nostrud exerci tation ullamcorper suscipit lobortis nisl ut aliquip ex consequat. Duis uat, vel illum nulla odio dignissim qui blandit praesent luptatum zzril delim ad minim veniam, quis nostrud ullamcorper suscipit lobortis nisl ut aliquip ex ea commodo consequat.
Duis te feugait nulla facilisi. Lorem ipsum dolor sit amet, consectetuer adipiscing elit, sed

diam nonummy nibh euismod tincidunt dolore magna aliquam erat volutpat.
Ut wisi enim ad minim veniam, im ad minim veniam, quis nostrud exerci tation ullamcorper suscipit lobortis nisl ut aliquip ex ea commodo consequat. Duis te feugait nulla facilisi. Lorem ipsum dolor sit amet, consectetuer adminim veniam.
Quis nostrudexer citation orper suscipit lobortis nisl ut aliquip ex consequat. Duis autem vel eum iriure dolor velit esse molestie consequat, vel illum dolore eu feugiipiscing elit, sed diam nonummy nibh euismod tincidunt ut laoreet ullamcorper suscipit lobortis nisl ut aliquip ex ea commodo consequat. Duis autem vel eum iriure dolim ad minim veniam, quis nostrud exerci tation ullamcorper suscipit lobortis nisl ut aliquip ex ea commodo

Every typeface has its own color. Squint at this page and see the variety of grays created by these familiar fonts.

Lorem ipsum dolor sit amet, consectetuer adipiscing elit, sed diam nonummy nibh euismod tincidunt ut laoreet dolore magna aliquam erat volutpat. Ut wisi enim ad minim veniam, quis nostrud exerci tation ullamcorper suscipit lobortis nisl ut aliquip ex ea commodo consequat. Duis te feugifacilisi. Lorem ipsum dolor sit amet, consectetuer adipiscing elit, nibh euismod.

Ut wisi enim ad minim veniam, quis nostrud exerci tation ullamcorper suscipit lobortis nisl ut aliquip ex ea commodo consequat. Duis autem dolor in hendrerit in vulputate velit esse molestie consequat, vel illum dolore eu feugiat nulla facilisis at vero eros et accumsan et iusto odio dignissim qui blandit praesent luptatum zzril delenit augue duis dolore te feugait nulla facilisi. Lorem ipsum dolor sit amet, consectetuer

Lorem ipsum dolor sit amet, consectetuer adipiscing elit, sed diam nonummy nibh euismod tincidunt ut laoreet dolore magna aliquam erat volutpat. Ut wisi enim ad minim veniam, quis nostrud exerci tation ullamcorper suscipit lobortis nisl ut aliquip ex ea commodo consequat. Duis te feugifacilisi. Lorem ipsum dolor sit amet, consectetuer adipiscing elit, nibh euismod.

Ut wisi enim ad minim veniam, quis nostrud exerci tation ullamcorper suscipit lobortis nisl ut aliquip ex ea commodo consequat. Duis autem dolor in hendrerit in vulputate velit esse molestie consequat, vel illum dolore eu feugiat nulla facilisis at vero eros et accumsan et iusto odio dignissim qui blandit praesent luptatum zzril delenit augue duis dolore te feugait nulla facilisi. Lorem ipsum dolor sit amet, consectetuer adipiscing elit, sed diam nonummy nibh euismod tincidunt ut laoreet dolore magna aliquam erat volutpat. Ut wisi enim ad minim veniam, quis nostrud suscipit lobortis nisl ut aliquip ex ea commodo consequat.

Lorem ipsum dolor sit amet, consectetuer adipiscing elit, sed diam nonummy nibh euismod tincidunt ut laoreet dolore magna aliquam erat volutpat. Ut wisi enim ad minim veniam, quis nostrud exerci tation ullamcorper suscipit lobortis nisl ut aliquip ex ea commodo consequat. Duis te feugifacilisi. Lorem ipsum dolor sit amet, consectetuer adipiscing elit, nibh euismod.

Ut wisi enim ad minim veniam, quis nostrud exerci tation ullamcorper suscipit lobortis nisl ut aliquip ex ea commodo consequat. Duis autem dolor in hendrerit in vulputate velit esse molestie consequat, vel illum dolore eu feugiat nulla facilisis at vero eros et accumsan et iusto odio dignissim qui blandit praesent luptatum zzril delenit augue duis dolore te feugait nulla facilisi. Lorem ipsum dolor sit amet, consectetuer adipiscing elit, sed diam nonummy nibh euismod tincidunt ut laoreet dolore magna aliquam erat volutpat. Ut wisi enim ad minim veniam, quis nostrud suscipit lobortis nisl ut aliquip ex ea commodo consequat.

Frutiger Black

Garamond Condensed

Bodoni

Lorem ipsum dolor sit amet, consectetuer adipiscing elit, sed diam nonummy nibh euismod tincidunt ut laoreet dolore magna aliquam erat volutpat. Ut wisi enim ad minim veniam, quis nostrud exerci tation ullamcorper suscipit lobortis nisl ut aliquip ex ea commodo consequat. Duis te feugifacilisi. Lorem ipsum dolor sit amet, consectetuer adipiscing elit, nibh euismod.

Ut wisi enim ad minim veniam, quis nostrud exerci tation ullamcorper suscipit lobortis nisl ut aliquip ex ea commodo consequat. Duis autem dolor in hendrerit in vulputate velit esse molestie consequat, vel illum dolore eu feugiat nulla facilisis at vero eros et accumsan et iusto odio dignissim qui blandit praesent luptatum zzril delenit augue duis dolore te feugait nulla facilisi. Lorem ipsum dolor sit amet, consectetuer adipiscing elit, sed diam nonummy nibh euismod tincidunt ut laoreet dolore magna aliquam erat volutpat. Ut wisi enim ad minim veniam, quis nostrud suscipit lobortis nisl ut aliquip ex ea commodo consequat.

Lorem ipsum dolor sit amet, consectetuer adipiscing elit, sed diam nonummy nibh euismod tincidunt ut laoreet dolore magna aliquam erat volutpat. Ut wisi enim ad minim veniam, quis nostrud exerci tation ullamcorper suscipit lobortis nisl ut aliquip ex ea commodo consequat. Duis te feugifacilisi. Lorem ipsum dolor sit amet, consectetuer adipiscing elit, nibh euismod.

Ut wisi enim ad minim veniam, quis nostrud exerci tation ullamcorper suscipit lobortis nisl ut aliquip ex ea commodo consequat. Duis autem dolor in hendrerit in vulputate velit esse molestie consequat, vel illum dolore eu feugiat nulla facilisis at vero eros et accumsan et iusto odio dignissim qui blandit praesent luptatum zzril delenit augue duis dolore te feugait nulla facilisi. Lorem ipsum dolor sit amet, consectetuer adipiscing elit, sed diam nonummy nibh euismod tincidunt ut laoreet dolore magna aliquam erat volutpat. Ut wisi enim ad minim veniam, quis nostrud suscipit lobortis nisl ut aliquip ex ea commodo consequat.

Lorem ipsum dolor sit amet, consectetuer adipiscing elit, sed diam nonummy nibh euismod tincidunt ut laoreet dolore magna aliquam erat volutpat. Ut wisi enim ad minim veniam, quis nostrud exerci tation ullamcorper suscipit lobortis nisl ut aliquip ex ea commodo consequat. Duis te feugifacilisi. Lorem ipsum dolor sit amet, consectetuer adipiscing elit, nibh euismod.

Ut wisi enim ad minim veniam, quis nostrud exerci tation ullamcorper suscipit lobortis nisl ut aliquip ex ea commodo consequat. Duis autem dolor in hendrerit in vulputate velit esse molestie consequat, vel illum dolore eu feugiat nulla facilisis at vero eros et accumsan et iusto odio dignissim qui blandit praesent luptatum zzril delenit augue duis dolore te feugait nulla facilisi. Lorem ipsum dolor sit amet, consectetuer adipiscing elit, sed diam nonummy nibh euismod tincidunt ut laoreet dolore magna aliquam erat volutpat. Ut wisi enim ad minim veniam, quis nostrud suscipit lobortis nisl ut aliquip ex ea commodo consequat.

Futura

Helvetica Compressed

Baskerville

Size Contrast

Another way of grabbing the reader's attention is by dramatically varying the size of the elements on the page. With type, for example, it's possible to make an ordinary headline extraordinary by enlarging a single letter or word.

Although you'll want to keep your headlines at a large, readable size, extra-large or relatively small type can sometimes provide attention-getting results. The large type gets noticed simply because of its size. When surrounded by a lot of white space, a smaller headline or graphic draws attention immediately. (The old Volkswagen "Think Small" campaign—with an inch-high VW on a nearly blank full page—is an excellent example of this technique.)

The greatly enlarged ampersand adds a vigorous dynamic to this otherwise ordinary page. If the word "and" were used instead, it would be significantly less effective.

TODAY

TOMORROW

T O D A Y

at vero eros et accumsan et iusto odio dignissim qui blandit praesent luptatum zzril delenit augue duis dolore te feugait nulla facilisi. Lorem ipsum dolor sit amet, consectetuer adipiscing elit, sed diam nonummy nibh euismod tincidunt ut laoreet dolore magna aliqat. Ut wisi enim ad minim veniam, quis nostrud exerci tation ullamcorper suscipit lobortis nisl ut aliquip ex ea commodo consequat. Duis te feugifacilisi. Loremat. Ut wisi enim ad minim veniam, quis nostrud exerci tation ullamcorper suscipit lobortis nisl ut aliquip ex ea commodo consequat. Duis te feugifacilisi. Lorem ipsum dolor sit amet,

consectetuer adipiscing elit, nibh euismod. Ut wisi enim ad minim veniam, quis nostrud exerci tation ullamcorper suscipit lobortis nisl ut aliquip ex ea commodo c ipsum dolor sit amet, consectetuer adipiscing elit, nibh euismod. Ut wisi enim ad minim veniam, quis nostrud exerci tation ullamcorper suscipit lobortis nisl ut aliquip ex ea commodo cuam

erat volutpat. Ut wisiat. Ut wisi enim ad minim veniam, quis nostrud exerci tation ullamcorper suscipit lobortis nisl ut aliquip ex ea commodo consequat. Duis te feugifacilisi. Lorem ipsum dolor sit amet, consectetuer adipiscing elit, nibh euismod. Ut wisi enim ad minim veniam, quis nostrud exerci tation ullamcorper suscipit lobortis nisl ut aliquip ex ea commodo

T O M O R R O W

Lorem ipsum dolor sit amet, consectetuer adipiscing elit, sed diam nonummy nibh euismod tincidunt ut laoreet dolore magna aliquam erat volutpat. Ut wisi enim ad minim veniam, quis nostrud exerci tation ullamcorper suscipit lobortis nisl ut aliquip ex ea commodo consequat. Duis te feugifacilisi. Lorem ipsum dolor sit amet, consectetuer adipiscing elit, nibh euismod. Ut wisi enim ad minim veniam, quis nostrud exerci tation ullamcorper suscipit lobortis nisl ut aliquip ex ea commodo consequat. Duis autem dolor in hendrerit in vulputate velit esse molestie consequat, vel illum dolore eu feugiat nulla facilisis

How can a store this small have a sale this big?

Lorem ipsum dolor sit amet, consectetuer adipiscing elit, sed diam nonummy nibh euismod tincidunt ut laoreet dolore magna aliquam erat volutpat. Ut wisi enim ad minim veniam, quis nostrud exerci tation ullamcorper suscipit lobortis nisl ut aliquip ex ea commodo consequat. Duis te feugifacilisi. Lorem ipsum dolor sit amet, consectetuer adipiscing elit, nibh euismod.

Ut wisi enim ad minim veniam, quis nostrud exerci tation ullamcorper suscipit lobortis nisl ut aliquip ex ea commodo consequat. Duis autem dolor in hendrerit in vulputate velit esse molestie consequat, vel illum dolore eu feugiat nulla facilisis at vero eros et accumsan et iusto odio dignissim qui blandit praesent luptatum zzril delenit augue duis dolore te feugait nulla facilisi. Lorem ipsum dolor sit amet, consectetuer adipiscing elit, sed diam nonummy nibh euismod tincidunt ut laoreet dolore magna aliquam erat volutpat. Ut wisi enim ad minim veniam, quis nostrud suscipit lobortis nisl ut aliquip ex ea commodo consequat.

THE LITTLE HOUSE ON THE PARKING LOT

How can a store this small have a sale this big?

Lorem ipsum dolor sit amet, consectetuer adipiscing elit, sed diam nonummy nibh euismod tincidunt ut laoreet dolore magna aliquam erat volutpat. Ut wisi enim ad minim veniam, quis nostrud exerci tation ullamcorper suscipit lobortis nisl ut aliquip ex ea commodo consequat. Duis te feugifacilisi. Lorem ipsum dolor sit amet, consectetuer adipiscing elit,

nibh euismod.
Ut wisi enim ad minim veniam, quis nostrud exerci tation ullamcorper suscipit lobortis nisl ut aliquip ex ea commodo c

THE LITTLE HOUSE ON THE PARKING LOT

How can a store this small have a sale this big?

These three versions of the same ad use varying sizes of the same headline. The one in the upper left uses a typical headline size. The large type in the upper right sample gets noticed simply because of its size. At left, the small type works well because the surrounding white space draws your attention to the headline. Which of the three is most effective? Also take note of exactly how your eye scans each advertisement.

Lorem ipsum dolor sit amet, consectetuer adipiscing elit, sed diam nonummy nibh euismod tincidunt ut laoreet dolore magna aliquam erat volutpat. Ut wisi enim ad minim veniam, qmcorper suscipit lobortis nisl ut ex ea commodo consequat. Duis te feugifacilisi. Lorem ipsum nsectetuer adipiscing elit, nibh euismod.uis nostrud exerci tation ullamcorper suscipit lobortis nisl ut aliquip ex ea commodo consequat. Duis te feugifacilisi. Lorem ipsum dolor sit amet,

consectetuer adipiscing elit, nibh euismod.
Ut wisi enim ad minim veniam, quis nostrud exerci tation ullamcorper suscipit lobortis nisl ut aliquip ex e commodo c

THE LITTLE HOUSE ON THE PARKING LOT

SAY
CAN YOU SEE?

If not, maybe it's
time to take
advantage of
LensBenders 4th
of July weekend
special on
prescription
sunglasses

STORES ARE OPEN UNTIL 6PM AT WENSLEYDALE, AIRDALE, AND CHIPPENDALE

(Far left) The capital O is a real attention-getter. The reader's eye is hooked by its size and drawn through the rest of the copy.

(Left) The reader's eye moves in a clockwise manner, starting at the largest item on the page, moving across to the smaller speaker, down to the headline and finally over to the copy. What makes this ad work is the contrasting size of the speakers.

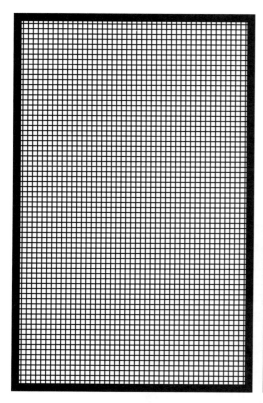

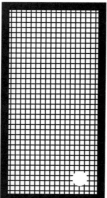

Lorem ipsum dolor sit amet, consectetuer adipiscing elit, sed diam nonummy nibh euismod tincidunt ut laoreet dolore magna aliquam erat volutpat. Ut wisi enim ad minim veniam, quis nostrud exerci tation ullamcorper suscipit lobortis nisl ut aliquip ex ea commodo consequat. Duis te feugifacilisi. Lorem ipsum dolor sit amet, consectetuer adipiscing elit, nibh euismod.
Ut wisi enim ad minim veniam, quis nostrud exerci tation ullamcorper suscipit lobortis nisl ut aliquip ex ea commodo consequat. Duis autem dolor in hendrerit in vulputate velit esse molestie consequat, vel illum dolore eu feugiat nulla facilisis at vero

TWICE THE SOUND. HALF THE SIZE.

Weight Contrast

Weight contrast—usually defined as a "thick/thin" or "heavy/light" relationship—is readily seen in type. The most ubiquitous example is **bold** type, due in part to the proliferation of personal computers. If there are too many bold elements, none will get noticed. Save the bold type for headlines and subheads and use *italics* for emphasis in body copy.

Another example of ineffective use of the weight contrast technique occurs when one element is overwhelmed by another, obscuring the message or rendering one of the design elements practically invisible.

This example illustrates effective heavy/light contrast. The thin lines provide good contrast to the heavy block of reversed type, creating a visually interesting design.

CASH & CARRY

Gardening Department
Price List 1992

SLIMMER

The diet program with a difference

SLIMMER

The diet program with a difference

LINK LIGHT
A new concept in bulb design

Outlining can be used to create a lighter look with the same typeface. Use sparingly!

In the top example, the heavy-versus-light contrast of the type in the "Slimmer" logo forms a kind of pleasing visual pun—the individual letters get thinner as if they, too, have been transformed by a weight-loss program. The second version of the Slimmer logo not only doesn't make visual sense (who wants a radically fluctuating diet program?), but is difficult to read.

**First
Federal
Mortgage**

(Above and left) Contrasts
in line weight are often
found in the simple,
repeated shapes of
corporate symbols.

sunset
tours

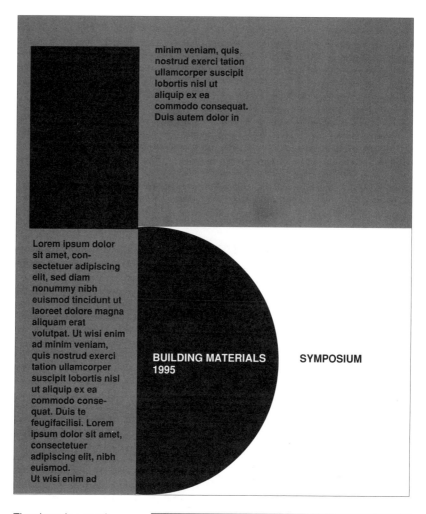

minim veniam, quis nostrud exerci tation ullamcorper suscipit lobortis nisl ut aliquip ex ea commodo consequat. Duis autem dolor in

Lorem ipsum dolor sit amet, consectetuer adipiscing elit, sed diam nonummy nibh euismod tincidunt ut laoreet dolore magna aliquam erat volutpat. Ut wisi enim ad minim veniam, quis nostrud exerci tation ullamcorper suscipit lobortis nisl ut aliquip ex ea commodo consequat. Duis te feugifacilisi. Lorem ipsum dolor sit amet, consectetuer adipiscing elit, nibh euismod. Ut wisi enim ad

BUILDING MATERIALS 1995   **SYMPOSIUM**

The above is a good example of shape contrast. Not only is the design visually pleasing and entertaining to the eye, but it leads the viewer from the upper left of the page (where the eye automatically begins to read) to the title at the lower right.

Shape Contrast

Judicious use of curved and straight elements is an excellent way to lead readers through your material.

Another dramatic visual effect occurs when a freeform object is juxtaposed with a more geometric one. The readers are startled by the contrast and immediately are drawn to the area of greatest contrast.

The example on the opposite page—and many other samples throughout this book—make use of repetition as a design technique. Used in conjunction with the contrasting principles outlined in this section, repetition lends harmony and continuity to a page design.

(Far right) The curved body shapes contrast nicely with the angular intersecting planes. This juxtaposition causes the eye to "dance" around the design.

(Right) The repeating curved shape of the egg is literally broken by the one with the jagged crack. Note how the eye goes first to the egg with the crack and follows the crack to the headline.

Breakthrough

Changing behavior patterns with exercise, diet and meditation

**improvisational
dance
theatre
workshop**

In the example at right, the eye can't help but be drawn to the area of contrast; in this case, the larger, unreversed "5."

Five ways to enhance your investment portfolio

Ut wisi enim ad minim veniam, quis nostrud exerci tation ullamcorper suscipit lobortis nisl ut aliquip ex ea commodo consequat.
Autem vel eum iriure dolor in hendrerit in vulputate velit esse
molestie consequat, vel illum dolore eu feugiat nulla facilisis at vero
eros et accumsan et iusto odio dignissim qui blandit praesent
luptatum zzril delenit augue duis dolore te feugait nulla facilisi.

Position Contrast

There are two basic kinds of position contrast. The first is achieved by removing or duplicating an object that's part of a group. The second is achieved by rotating type or graphics at an angle.

When you pull out an item that's part of a group, you create visual appeal. In a tall column of horizontal lines, you notice the space where one of the lines is missing. (This effect also involves some *repetition*.) Or you can duplicate one of the lines and move it to the side. The eye will naturally flow to that spot.

(Right) Removing or duplicating an object that's part of a group creates visual appeal. In this sample, a few trees were removed from the group. The group was then copied, reduced and placed where one of the original trees had been removed.

Forest
Restoration
Techniques
Conference
94

(Below) In this example, a single triangle was duplicated, resized and repositioned to achieve this forward-moving image.

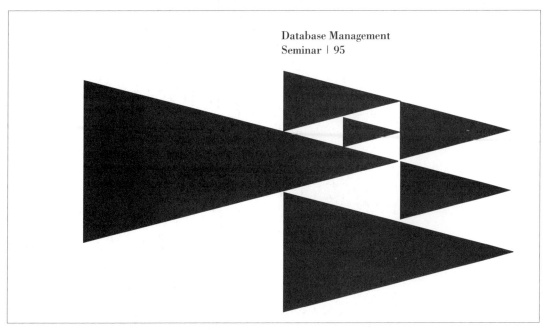

Database Management
Seminar | 95

Another example of position contrast is placing photos and illustrations at an angle on the page. These tilted elements add variety to the page and provide welcome contrast to the usual horizontal rows of text. Type at an angle is effective, too, provided it's used sparingly. Too much angled copy is difficult to read.

Lorem ipsum dolor sit amet, consectetuer adipiscing elit, sed diam nonummy nibh euismod tincidunt ut laoreet dolore magna aliquam erat volutpat. Ut wisi enim ad minim veniam, quis nostrud exerci tation ullamcorper suscipit lobortis nisl ut aliquip ex ea commodo consequat. Duis te feugifacilisi. Lorem ipsum dolor sit amet, consectetuer adipiscing elit, nibh euismod.

Ut wisi enim ad minim veniam, quis nostrud exerci tation ullamcorper suscipit lobortis nisl ut aliquip ex ea commodo consequat. Duis autem dolor in hendrerit in vulputate velit esse molestie consequat, vel illum dolore eu feuLorem ipsum dolor sit amet, consectetuer adipiscing elit, sed diam nonummy nibh euismod tincidunt ut laoreet dolore magna aliquam erat volutpat. Ut wisi enim ad minim veniam, quis nostrud exerci tation ullamcorper suscipit lobortis nisl ut aliquip ex ea commodo consequat. Duis te feugifacilisi. Lorem ipsum dolor sit amet, consectetuer adipiscing elit, nibh euismod.

Ut wisi enim ad minim veniam, quis nostrud exerci tation ullamcorper suscipit lobortis nisl ut aliquip ex ea commodo consequat. Duis autem dolor in hendrerit in vulputate velit esse molestie consequat, vel illum dolore eu feugiat nulla facilisis at vero eros et accumsan et iusto odio dignissim qui blandit praesent luptatum zzril delenit augue duis dolore te feugait nulla facilisi. Lorem ipsum dolor sit amet, consectetuer adipiscing elit, sed diam nonummy nibh euismod tincidunt ut laoreet dolore magna aliquam erat volutpat. Ut wisi enim ad minim veniam, qgiat nulla facilisis at vero eros et accumsan et iusto odio dignissim qui blandit praesent luptatum zzril delenit augue duis dolore te feugait nulla facilisi. Lorem ipsum dolor sit amet, consectetuer adipiscing elit, sed diam nonummy nibh euismod tincidunt ut laoreet

dolore magna aliquam erat volutpat. Ut wisi enim ad minim veniam, quis nquam erat volutpat. Ut wisi enim ad minim veniam, quis nostrud exerci tation ullamcorper suscipit lobortis nisl ut aliquip ex ea commodo consequat. Duis te feugifacilisi. Lorem ipsum dolor sit amet, consectetuer adipiscing elit, nibh euismod.

Ut wisi enim ad minim veniam, quis nostrud exerci tation ullamcorper suscipit lobortis nisl ut aliquip ex ea commodo consequat. Duis autem dolor in hendrerit in vulputate velit esse molestie consequat, vel illum dolore eu feu Lorem ipsum dolor sit amet, consectetuer adipiscing elit, sed diam nonummy nibh euismod tincidunt ut laoreet dolore magna aliquam erat volutpat. Ut wisi enim ad minim veniam, quis nostrud exerci tation ullamcorper suscipit lobortis nisl ut aliquip ex ea commodo consequat. Duis te feugifacilisi. Lorem ipsum dolor sit amet, consectetuer adipiscing elit, nibh euismod.

Ut wisi enim ad minim veniam, quis nostrud exerci tation ullamcorper suscipit lobortis nisl ut aliquip ex ea commodo consequat. Duis autem dolor in hendrerit in vulputate velit esse molestie consequat, vel illum dolore eu feugiat nulla facilisis at vero eros et accumsan et iusto odio dignissim qui blandit praesent luptatum zzril delenit augue duis dolore te feugait nulla facilisi. Lorem ipsum dolor sit amet, consectetuer adipiscing elit, sed diam nonummy nibhostrud suscipit lobortis nisl ut aliquip ex ea commodo consequat.

Lorem ipsum dolor sit amet, consectetuer adipiscing elit, sed diam nonummy nibh euismod tincidunt ut laoreet dolore magna aliquam erat volutpat. Ut wisi enim ad minim veniam, quis nostrud exerci tation ullamcorper suscipit lobortis nisl ut aliquip ex ea commodo consequat. Duis te feugifacilisi. Lorem ipsum dolor sit amet, consectetuer adipiscing elit, nibh euismod.

Ut wisi enim ad minim veniam, quis nostrud exerci tation ullamcorper suscipit lobortis nisl ut aliquip ex ea commodo consequat. Duis autem dolor in hendrerit in vulputate velit esse molestie consequat, vel illum dolore eu feugiat nulla facilisis at

vero eros et accumsan et iusto odio dignissim qui blandit praesent luptatum zzril delenit augue duis dolore te feugait nulla facilisi. Lorem ipsum dolor sit amet, consectetuer adipiscing elit, sed diam nonummy nibhrem ipsum dolor sit amet, consectetuer adipiscing elit, sed diam nonummy nibh euismod tincidunt ut laoreet dolore magna aliquam erat volutpat. Ut wisi enim ad minim veniam, quis nostrud exerci tation ullamcorper suscipit lobortis nisl ut aliquip ex ea commodo consequat. Duis autem dolor in hendrerit in vulputate velit esse molestie consequat, vel illum dolore eu feuLorem ipsum dolor sit amet, consectetuer adipiscing elit, sed diam nonummy nibh euismod tincidunt ut laoreet dolore magna aliquam erat volutpat. Ut wisi enim ad minim veniam, quis nostrud exerci tation ullamcorper suscipit lobortis nisl ut aliquip ex ea commodo consequat. Duis autem dolor in hendrerit in vulputate velit esse molestie consequat, vel illum dolore eu feugiat nulla facilisis at vero eros et accumsan et iusto odio dignissim qui blandit praesent luptatum zzril delenit augue duis dolore te feugait nulla facilisi. Lorem ipsum dolor sit amet, consectetuer adipiscing elit, sed diam nonummy nibh euismod tincidunt ut laoreet dolore magna aliquam erat volutpat. Ut wisi enim ad minim veniam, quis nostrud suscipit lobortis nisl ut aliquip ex ea commodo consequat.

Lorem ipsum dolor sit amet, consectetuer adipiscing elit, sed diam nonummy nibh euismod tincidunt ut laoreet dolore magna aliquam erat volutpat. Ut wisi enim ad minim veniam, quis nostrud exerci tation ullamcorper suscipit lobortis nisl ut aliquip ex ea commodo consequat. Duis te feugifacilisi. Lorem ipsum dolor sit amet, consectetuer adipiscing elit, nibh euismod. Ut wisi enim ad minim veniam, quis nostrud exerci tation ullamcorper suscipit lobortis nisl ut aliquip ex ea commodo consequat. Duis autem dolor in hendrerit in vulputate velit esse molestie consequat, vel illum dolore eu feuLorem ipsum dolor sit amet, consectetuer adipiscing elit, sed diam nonummy nibh euismod tincidunt ut laoreet dolore magna aliquam erat volutpat. Ut wisi enim ad minim veniam, quis nostrud exerci tation ullamcorper suscipit lobortis nisl ut aliquip ex ea commodo consequat. Duis te feugifacilisi. Lorem ipsum dolor Ut wisi enim ad minim veniam, quis nostrud exerci tation ullamcorper suscipit lobortis nisl ut aliquip ex ea commodo consequat. Duis autem dolor in hendrerit in vulputate velit esse molestie consequat, vel illum dolore eu feugiat nulla facilisis at vero eros et accumsan et iusto odio dignissim qui blandit praesent luptatum zzril delenit augue duis dolore te feugait nulla facilisi. Lorem ipsum dolor sit amet, consectetuer adipiscing elit, sed diam nonummy nibh euismod tincidunt ut laoreet dolore magna aliquam erat volutpat. Ut wisi enim ad minim veniam, qgiat nulla facilisis at vero eros et accumsan et iusto odio dignissim qui blandit praesent luptatum zzril delenit augue duis dolore te feugait nulla facilisi. Lorem ipsum dolor sit amet, consectetuer adipiscing elit, sed diam nonummy nibh euismod tincidunt ut laoreet dolore magna aliquam erat volutpat. Ut wisi enim ad minim veniam, quis nostrud suscipit lobortis nisl ut aliquip ex ea commodo consequat.

Some page-layout programs let you rotate type or objects. An angled element can contrast nicely with the typical horizontal rows of text. All samples on this spread show effective use of angled type, except the one directly below—it's too difficult to read the large amount of angled copy.

Dyslexia

12 Reasons Why Johnny Can't Spell

Lorem ipsum dolor sit amet, consectetuer adipiscing elit, sed diam nonummy nibh euismod tincidunt ut laoreet dolore magna aliquam erat volutpat. Ut wisi enim ad minim veniam, quis nostrud exerci tation ullamcorper suscipit lobortis nisl ut aliquip ex ea commodo consequat. Duis te feugifacilisi. Lorem ipsum dolor sit amet, consectetuer adipiscing elit, nibh euismod. Ut wisi enim ad minim veniam, quis nostrud exerci tation ullamcorper suscipit lobortis nisl ut aliquip ex ea commodo consequat. Duis autem dolor in hendrerit in vulputate velit esse molestie consequat, vel illum dolore eu feuLorem ipsum dolor sit amet, consectetuer adipiscing elit, sed diam nonummy nibh euismod tincidunt ut laoreet dolore magna aliquam erat volutpat. Ut wisi enim ad minim veniam, quis nostrud exerci tation ullamcorper suscipit lobortis nisl

ut aliquip ex ea commodo consequat. Duis autem dolor in hendrerit in vulputate velit esse molestie consequat, vel illum dolore eu feugiat nulla facilisis at vero eros et accumsan et iusto odio dignissim qui blandit praesent luptatum zzril delenit augue duis dolore te feugait nulla facilisi. Lorem ipsum dolor sit amet, consectetuer adipiscing elit, sed diam nonummy nibh euismod tincidunt ut laoreet dolore magna aliquam erat volutpat. Ut wisi enim ad minim veniam, qgiat nulla facilisis at vero eros et accumsan et iusto odio dignissim qui blandit praesent luptatum zzril delenit augue duis dolore te feugait nulla facilisi. Lorem ipsum dolor sit amet, consectetuer adipiscing elit, sed diam nonummy nibh euismod tincidunt ut laoreet dolore magna aliquam erat volutpat. Ut wisi enim ad minim veniam, quis nostrud suscipit lobortis nisl ut aliquip ex ea commodo consequat.

The Twelve Basic Causes of Dyslexia

Lorem ipsum dolor sit amet, consectetuer adipiscing elit, sed diam nonummy nibh euismod tincidunt ut laoreet dolore magna aliquam erat volutpat. Ut wisi enim ad minim veniam, quis nostrud exerci tation ullamcorper suscipit lobortis nisl ut aliquip ex ea commodo consequat. Duis te feugifacilisi. Lorem ipsum dolor sit amet, consectetuer adipiscing elit, nibh euismod. Ut wisi enim ad minim veniam, quis nostrud exerci tation ullamcorper suscipit lobortis nisl ut aliquip ex ea commodo consequat. Duis autem dolor in hendrerit in vulputate velit esse molestie consequat, vel illum dolore eu feuLorem ipsum dolor sit amet, consectetuer adipiscing elit, sed diam nonummy nibh euismod tincidunt ut laoreet dolore magna aliquam erat volutpat. Ut wisi enim ad minim veniam, quis nostrud exerci tation ullamcorper suscipit lobortis nisl ut aliquip ex ea commodo consequat. Duis te feugifacilisi. Lorem ipsum dolor sit amet, consectetuer adipiscing elit, nibh euismod. Ut wisi enim ad minim veniam, quis nostrud exerci tation ullamcorper suscipit lobortis nisl

ut aliquip ex ea commodo consequat. Duis autem dolor in hendrerit in vulputate velit esse molestie consequat, vel illum dolore eu feugiat nulla facilisis at vero eros et accumsan et iusto odio dignissim qui blandit praesent luptatum zzril delenit augue duis dolore te feugait nulla facilisi. Lorem ipsum dolor sit amet, consectetuer adipiscing elit, sed diam nonummy nibh euismod tincidunt ut laoreet dolore magna aliquam erat volutpat. Ut wisi enim ad minim veniam, quis nostrud suscipit lobortis nisl ut

Texture Contrast

Many computer programs can automatically generate black-and-white patterns that add a textured
appearance to your document. Perhaps you'll want
to create your own. In any case, use them with
restraint: patterns can easily overwhelm rather
than enhance the message.

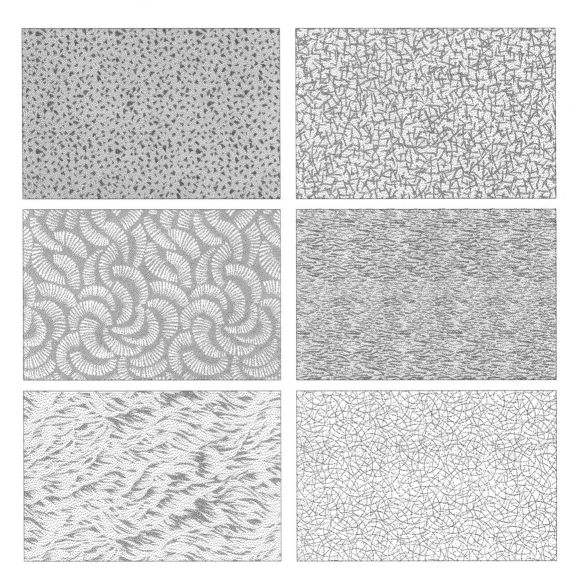

(Above) Which of the two examples shown allows the message to come through loud and clear?

(Left) Note how the small dot texture gives a gray appearance to this panel from a multimedia presentation. The pattern is lightened around the headline to make it more readable. Creative use of textures is explored in later chapters.

Too Much of a Good Thing

Probably the only mistake bigger than creating a boring page is designing one that's overly busy—too much "design" turns into so much junk. The reader will end up confused and uninformed. To be great, a page design needs to be "transparent"—that is, it can't draw too much attention to itself or it's not doing its job.

Follow the transformation of the rather boring newsletter layout below. Keep in mind the rule: use gray strategically—not randomly—to achieve the desired effect.

This newsletter is kind of boring and needs a little sprucing up...

Desktopper'sWeekly

Month Year Volume 00 Number 0

Macintosh font explosion hits home

Adipiscing elit sed diam nonummy nibh euismod tincidunt ut laoreet dolore magna aliquam erat volutpat. Ut wisi enim ad minim veniam, quis nostrud exercit tation ullamcorper suscipit lobortis nisl ut aliquip ex ea commodo consequat. Duis autem vel eum iriure dolor in hendrerit in vulputate velit esse molestie consequat, vel illum dolore eu feugiat nulla facilisis at vero eros et accumsan et iusto odio dignissum qui blandit praesent luptatum zzril delenit augue duis dolore te feugiat nulla facilisi. Lorem ipsum dolor sit amet, consectetuer adipiscing elit, sed daim nonummy nibh euismod tincidunt ut laoreet dolore magna aliquam erat volutpat. Ut wisi enim ad minim veniam, quis nostrud exerci tation ullamcorper suscipit lobortis nisl ut aliquip.

Duis autem vel eum iriure dolor in hendrerit in vulputate velit esse molestie consequat, vel illum dolore eu feugiat nulla facilisis at vero eros et accumsan et iusto odio dignissum qui blandit praesent luptatum zzril delenit augue duis dolore te feugiat nulla facilisi. Lorem ipsum dolor sit amet, consectetuer adipiscing elit, sed daim.

Lorem ipsum dolor sit amet, consectetuer adipiscing elit, sed daim nonummy nibh euismod tincidunt ut laoreet dolore magna aliquam erat volutpat. Ut wisi enim ad minim veniam, quis nostrud exerci tation ullamcorper suscipit lobortis nisl ut aliquip.

Duis autem vel eum iriure dolor in hendrerit in vulputate velit esse molestie consequat, vel illum dolore eu feugiat nulla facilisis at vero eros et accumsan et iusto odio

Contents

dignissum qui blandit praesent luptatum zzril delenit augue duis dolore te feugiat nulla facilisi. Lorem ipsum dolor sit amet, consectetuer adipiscing elit, sed daim.

Adipiscing elit, sed daim nonummy nibh euismod tincidunt ut laoreet dolore magna aliquam erat voluptat. Ut wisi enim ad minim veniam, quis nostrud exerci tation ullamcorper suscipit lobortis nisl ut aliquip..

Lorem ipsum dolor sit amet, consectetuer adipiscing elit, sed daim nonummy nibh euismod tincidunt ut laoreet dolore magna aliquam erat voluptat.

Prepress links better than ever

Adipiscing elit sed diam nonummy nibh euismod tincidunt ut laoreet dolore magna aliquam erat volutpat. Ut wisi enim ad minim veniam, quis nostrud exercit tation ullamcorper suscipit lobortis nisl ut aliquip ex ea commodo consequat. Duis autem vel eum iriure dolor in hendrerit in vulputate velit esse molestie consequat, vel illum dolore eu feugiat nulla facilisis at vero eros et accumsan et iusto odio dignissum qui blandit praesent luptatum zzril delenit augue duis dolore te feugiat nulla facilisi. Lorem ipsum dolor sit amet, consectetuer adipiscing elit, sed daim nonummy nibh euismod tincidunt ut laoreet dolore magna aliquam erat voluptat. Ut wisi enim ad minim veniam, quis nostrud exerci tation ullamcorper suscipit lobortis nisl ut aliquip.

Duis autem vel eum iriure dolor in hendrerit in vulputate velit esse molestie consequat, vel illum dolore eu feugiat nulla facilisis at vero eros et accumsan et iusto odio dignissum qui blandit praesent luptatum zzril delenit augue duis dolore te feugiat nulla facilisi. Lorem ipsum dolor sit amet, consectetuer adipiscing elit, sed daim.

Lorem ipsum dolor sit amet, consectetuer adipiscing elit, sed daim nonummy nibh euismod tincidunt ut laoreet dolore magna aliquam erat voluptat. Ut wisi enim ad minim veniam, quis nostrud exerci tation ullamcorper suscipit lobortis nisl ut aliquip.

Duis autem vel eum iriure dolor in hendrerit in vulputate velit esse molestie consequat, vel illum dolore eu feugiat nulla facilisis at vero eros et accumsan et iusto odio dignissum qui blandit praesent luptatum zzril delenit augue

Reversing two elements
on the page and adding a
few rules make it a little
more pleasant to look at ...

Desktopper'sWeekly

Month Year Volume 00 Number 0

Macintosh font explosion hits home

Adipiscing elit sed diam nonummy nibh eusimod tincidunt ut laoreet dolore magna aliquam erat volutpat. Ut wisi enim ad minim veniam, quis nostrud exercit tation ullamcorper suscipit lobortis nisl ut aliquip ex ea commodo consequat. Duis autem vel eum iriure dolor in hendrerit in vulputate velit esse molestie consequat, vel illum dolore eu feugiat nulla facilisis at vero eros et accumsan et iusto odio dignissum qui blandit praesent luptatum zzril delenit augue duis dolore te feugiat nulla facilisi. Lorem ipsum dolor sit amet, consectetuer adipiscing elit, sed daim nonummy nibh euismod tincidunt ut laoreet dolore magna aliquam erat volutpat. Ut wisi enim ad minim veniam, quis nostrud exerci tation ullamcorper suscipit lobortis nisl ut aliquip.

Duis autem vel eum iriure dolor in hendrerit in vulputate velit esse molestie consequat, vel illum dolore eu feugiat nulla facilisis at vero eros et accumsan et iusto odio dignissum qui blandit praesent luptatum zzril delenit augue duis dolore te feugiat nulla facilisi. Lorem ipsum dolor sit amet, consectetuer adipiscing elit, sed daim.

Lorem ipsum dolor sit amet, consectetuer adipiscing elit, sed daim nonummy nibh euismod tincidunt ut laoreet dolore magna aliquam erat volutpat. Ut wisi enim ad minim veniam, quis nostrud exerci tation ullamcorper suscipit lobortis nisl ut aliquip.

Duis autem vel eum iriure dolor in hendrerit in vulputate velit esse molestie consequat, vel illum dolore eu feugiat nulla facilisis at vero eros et accumsan et iusto odio

Contents

dignissum qui blandit praesent luptatum zzril delenit augue duis dolore te feugiat nulla facilisi. Lorem ipsum dolor sit amet, consectetuer adipiscing elit, sed daim.

Adipiscing elit, sed daim nonummy nibh euismod tincidunt ut laoreet dolore magna aliquam erat volutpat. Ut wisi enim ad minim veniam, quis nostrud exerci tation ullamcorper suscipit lobortis nisl ut aliquip..

Lorem ipsum dolor sit amet, consectetuer adipiscing elit, sed daim nonummy nibh euismod tincidunt ut laoreet dolore magna aliquam erat volutpat.

Prepress links better than ever

Adipiscing elit sed diam nonummy nibh eusimod tincidunt ut laoreet dolore magna aliquam erat volutpat. Ut wisi enim ad minim veniam, quis nostrud exercit tation ullamcorper suscipit lobortis nisl ut aliquip ex ea commodo consequat. Duis autem vel eum iriure dolor in hendrerit in vulputate velit esse molestie consequat, vel illum dolore eu feugiat nulla facilisis at vero eros et accumsan et iusto odio dignissum qui blandit praesent luptatum zzril delenit augue duis dolore te feugiat nulla facilisi. Lorem ipsum dolor sit amet, consectetuer adipiscing elit, sed daim nonummy nibh euismod tincidunt ut laoreet dolore magna aliquam erat volutpat. Ut wisi enim ad minim veniam, quis nostrud exerci tation ullamcorper suscipit lobortis nisl ut aliquip.

Duis autem vel eum iriure dolor in hendrerit in vulputate velit esse molestie consequat, vel illum dolore eu feugiat nulla facilisis at vero eros et accumsan et iusto odio dignissum qui blandit praesent luptatum zzril delenit augue duis dolore te feugiat nulla facilisi. Lorem ipsum dolor sit amet, consectetuer adipiscing elit, sed daim.

Lorem ipsum dolor sit amet, consectetuer adipiscing elit, sed daim nonummy nibh euismod tincidunt ut laoreet dolore magna aliquam erat volutpat. Ut wisi enim ad minim veniam, quis nostrud exerci tation ullamcorper suscipit lobortis nisl ut aliquip.

Duis autem vel eum iriure dolor in hendrerit in vulputate velit esse molestie consequat, vel illum dolore eu feugiat nulla facilisis at vero eros et accumsan et iusto odio dignissum qui blandit praesent luptatum zzril delenit augue

Then a shaded box and
an appropriate piece of
clip art can be added…

Desktopper's**Weekly**

Month Year Volume00 Number 0

Macintosh font explosion hits home

Lorem ipsum dolor sit amet, consectetuer adipiscing elit, sed diam nonummy nibh euismod tincidunt ut laoreet dolore magna aliquam erat volutpat. Ut wisi enim ad minim veniam, quis nostrud exerci tation ullamcorper suscipit lobortis nisl ut aliquip ex ea commodo consequat. Duis te feugifacilisi. Lorem ipsum dolor sit amet, consectetuer adipiscing elit, nibh euismod.

Lorem ipsum dolor sit amet, consectetuer adipiscing elit, sed diam nonummy nibh euismod tincidunt ut laoreet dolore magna aliquam erat volutpat. Ut wisi enim ad minim veniam, quis nostrud exerci tation ullamcorper suscipit lobortis nisl ut aliquip ex ea commodo consequat. Duis te feugifacilisi. Lorem ipsum dolor sit amet, consectetuer adipiscing elit, nibh euismod.

Ut wisi enim ad minim veniam, quis nostrud exerci tation ullamcorper suscipit lobortis nisl ut aliquip ex ea commodo consequat. Duis autem dolor in hendrerit in vulputate velit esse molestie consequat, vel illum dolore eu feugiat nulla facilisis at vero eros et accumsan et iusto odio dignissim qui blandit praesent luptatum zzril delenit augue duis dolore te feugait nulla facilisi. Lorem ipsum dolor sit amet, consectetuer adipiscing elit, sed diam nonummy nibh volutpat. Ut wisi enim ad minim veniam, quis nostrud suscipit lobortis nisl ut aliquip ex ea commodo consequat.

Lorem ipsum dolor sit amet, consectetuer adipiscing elit, sed diam nonummy nibh euismod tincidunt ut laoreet dolore magna aliquam erat volutpat. Ut wisi enim ad minim veniam, quis nostrud exerci tation ullamcorper suscipit lobortis nisl ut aliquip ex ea commodo consequat. Duis te feugifacilisi. Lorem ipsum dolor sit amet, consectetuer adipiscing elit, nibh euismod.

Ut wisi enim ad minim veniam, quis nostrud exerci tation ullamcorper suscipit lobortis nisl ut aliquip ex ea commodo

Contents

consequat. Duis autem dolor in hendrerit in vulputate velit esse molestie consequat, vel illum dolore eu feugiat nulla facilisis at vero eros et accumsan et iusto odio dignissim qui blandit praesent luptatum zzril delenit augue duis dolore te feugait nulla facilisi. Lorem ipsum dolor sit amet, consectetuer adipiscing elit, sed diam nonummy nibh euismod tincidunt ut laoreet dolore magna aliquam erat volutpat. Ut wisi enim ad minim veniam, quis nostrud

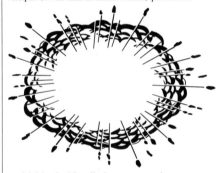

suscipit lobortis nisl ut aliquip ex ea commodo consequat.

Lorem ipsum dolor sit amet, consectetuer adipiscing elit, sed diam nonummy nibh euismod tincidunt ut laoreet dolore magna aliquam erat volutpat. Ut wisi enim ad minim veniam, quis nostrud exerci tation ullamcorper suscipit lobortis nisl ut aliquip ex ea commodo consequat. Duis te feugifacilisi. Lorem ipsum dolor sit amet, consectetuer adipiscing elit, nibh euismod.

Prepress links better than ever

Ut wisi enim ad minim veniam, quis nostrud exerci tation ullamcorper suscipit lobortis nisl ut aliquip ex ea commodo consequat. Duis autem dolor in hendrerit in vulputate velit esse molestie consequat, vel illum dolore eu feugiat nulla facilisis at vero eros et accumsan et iusto odio dignissim qui blandit praesent luptatum zzril delenit augue duis dolore te feugait nulla facilisi. Lorem ipsum dolor sit amet, consectetuer adipiscing elit, sed diam nonummy nibh euismod tincidunt ut laoreet dolore magna aliquam erat volutpat. Ut wisi enim ad minim veniam, quis nostrud suscipit lobortis nisl ut aliquip ex ea commodo consequat.

Next, drop caps to get
the reader involved.
Perfect! But...

Desktopper's**Weekly**

Month Year Volume00 Number 0

Macintosh font explosion hits home

Lorem ipsum dolor sit amet, consectetuer adipiscing elit, sed diam nonummy nibh euismod tincidunt ut laoreet dolore magna aliquam erat volutpat. Ut wisi enim ad minim veniam, quis nostrud exerci tation ullamcorper suscipit lobortis nisl ut aliquip ex ea commodo consequat. Duis te feugifacilisi. Lorem ipsum dolor sit amet, consectetuer adipiscing elit, nibh euismod.

Lorem ipsum dolor sit amet, consectetuer adipiscing elit, sed diam nonummy nibh euismod tincidunt ut laoreet dolore magna aliquam erat volutpat. Ut wisi enim ad minim veniam, quis nostrud exerci tation ullamcorper suscipit lobortis nisl ut aliquip ex ea commodo consequat. Duis te feugifacilisi. Lorem ipsum dolor sit amet, consectetuer adipiscing elit, nibh euismod.

Ut wisi enim ad minim veniam, quis nostrud exerci tation ullamcorper suscipit lobortis nisl ut aliquip ex ea commodo consequat. Duis autem dolor in hendrerit in vulputate velit esse molestie consequat, vel illum dolore eu feugiat nulla facilisis at vero eros et accumsan et iusto odio dignissim qui blandit praesent luptatum zzril delenit augue duis dolore te feugait nulla facilisi. Lorem ipsum dolor sit amet, consectetuer adipiscing elit, sed diam nonummy nibh volutpat. Ut wisi enim ad minim veniam, quis nostrud suscipit lobortis nisl ut aliquip ex ea commodo consequat.

Lorem ipsum dolor sit amet, consectetuer adipiscing elit, sed diam nonummy nibh euismod tincidunt ut laoreet dolore magna aliquam erat volutpat. Ut wisi enim ad minim veniam, quis nostrud exerci tation ullamcorper suscipit lobortis nisl ut aliquip ex ea commodo consequat. Duis te feugifacilisi. Lorem ipsum dolor sit amet, consectetuer adipiscing elit, nibh euismod.

Ut wisi enim ad minim veniam, quis nostrud exerci tation ullamcorper suscipit lobortis nisl ut aliquip ex ea commodo

Contents

consequat. Duis autem dolor in hendrerit in vulputate velit esse molestie consequat, vel illum dolore eu feugiat nulla facilisis at vero eros et accumsan et iusto odio dignissim qui blandit praesent luptatum zzril delenit augue duis dolore te feugait nulla facili. Lorem ipsum dolor sit amet, consectetuer adipiscing elit, sed diam nonummy nibh euismod tincidunt ut laoreet dolore magna aliquam erat volutpat. Ut wisi enim ad minim veniam, quis nostrud

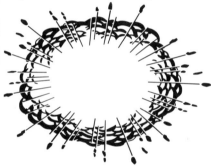

suscipit lobortis nisl ut aliquip ex ea commodo consequat.

Lorem ipsum dolor sit amet, consectetuer adipiscing elit, sed diam nonummy nibh euismod tincidunt ut laoreet dolore magna aliquam erat volutpat. Ut wisi enim ad minim veniam, quis nostrud exerci tation ullamcorper suscipit lobortis nisl ut aliquip ex ea commodo consequat. Duis te feugifacilisi. Lorem ipsum dolor sit amet, consectetuer adipiscing elit, nibh euismod.

Prepress links better than ever

Wisi enim ad minim veniam, quis nostrud exerci tation ullamcorper suscipit lobortis nisl ut aliquip ex ea commodo consequat. Duis autem dolor in hendrerit in vulputate velit esse molestie consequat, vel illum dolore eu feugiat nulla facilisis at vero eros et accumsan et iusto odio dignissim qui blandit praesent luptatum zzril delenit augue duis dolore te feugait nulla facili. Lorem ipsum dolor sit amet, consectetuer adipiscing elit, sed diam nonummy nibh euismod tincidunt ut laoreet dolore magna aliquam erat volutpat. Ut wisi enim ad minim veniam, quis nostrud suscipit lobortis nisl ut aliquip

...after more examples of contrast are added, the page below looks too busy. The reader is confused, not informed.

Desktopper'sWeekly

Month Year Volume00 Number 0

Macintosh font explosion hits home

Lorem ipsum dolor sit amet, consectetuer adipiscing elit, sed diam nonummy nibh euismod tincidunt ut laoreet dolore magna aliquam erat volutpat. Ut wisi enim ad minim veniam, quis nostrud exerci tation ullamcorper suscipit lobortis nisl ut aliquip ex ea commodo consequat. Duis te feugifacilisi. Lorem ipsum dolor sit amet, consectetuer adipiscing elit, nibh euismod.

Lorem ipsum dolor sit amet, consectetuer adipiscing elit, sed diam nonummy nibh euismod tincidunt ut laoreet dolore magna aliquam erat volutpat. Ut wisi enim ad minim veniam, quis nostrud exerci tation ullamcorper suscipit lobortis nisl ut

Ut wisi enim ad minim veniam, quis nostrud exerci tation ullamcorper suscipit lobortis nisl ut aliquip ex ea commodo consequat. Duis autem dolor in hendrerit in vulputate velit esse molestie consequat, vel illum dolore eu feugiat nulla facilisis at vero eros et accumsan et iusto odio dignissim qui blandit praesent luptatum zzril delenit augue duis dolore te feugait nulla facilisi. Lorem ipsum dolor sit amet, consectetuer adipiscing elit, sed diam nonummy nibh volutpat. Ut wisi enim ad minim veniam, quis nostrud suscipit lobortis nisl ut aliquip ex ea commodo consequat.

Lorem ipsum dolor sit amet, consectetuer adipiscing elit, sed diam nonummy nibh euismod tincidunt ut laoreet dolore magna aliquam erat volutpat. Ut wisi enim ad minim veniam, quis nostrud exerci tation ullamcorper suscipit lobortis nisl ut aliquip ex ea commodo consequat. Duis te feugifacilisi. Lorem ipsum dolor sit amet, consectetuer adipiscing elit, nibh euismod.

Ut wisi enim ad minim veniam, quis nostrud exerci tation ullamcorper suscipit lobortis nisl ut aliquip ex ea commodo consequat. Duis autem dolor in hendrerit in vulputate velit

Contents

esse molestie consequat, vel illum dolore eu feugiat nulla facilisis at vero eros et accumsan et iusto odio dignissim qui blandit praesent luptatum zzril delenit augue duis dolore te feugait nulla facili. Lorem ipsum dolor sit amet, consectetuer adipiscing elit, sed diam nonummy nibh euismod tincidunt ut laoreet dolore magna aliquam erat volutpat. Ut wisi enim ad minim veniam, quis nostrud suscipit lobortis nisl ut aliquip ex ea commodo consequat.

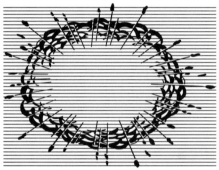

Lorem ipsum dolor sit amet, consectetuer adipiscing elit, sed diam nonummy nibh euismod tincidunt ut laoreet dolore magna aliquam erat volutpat. Ut wisi enim ad minim veniam, quis nostrud exerci tation ullamcorper suscipit lobortis nisl ut aliquip ex ea commodo consequat. Duis te feugifacilisi. Lorem ipsum dolor sit amet, consectetuer adipiscing elit, nibh euismod.

Prepress links better than ever

Wisi enim ad minim veniam, quis nostrud exerci tation ullamcorper suscipit lobortis nisl ut aliquip ex ea commodo consequat. Duis autem dolor in hendrerit in vulputate velit esse molestie consequat, vel illum dolore eu feugiat nulla facilisis at vero eros et accumsan et iusto odio dignissim qui blandit praesent luptatum zzril delenit augue duis dolore te feugait nulla facilisi. Lorem ipsum dolor sit amet, Ut wisi enim ad minim veniam, quis nostrud exerci tation ullamcorper suscipit lobortis nisl ut aliquip ex ea commodo consequat. Duis autem dolor in hendrerit in vulputate velit esse molestie consequat, vel illum dolore eu feugiat nulla facilisis at vero

Contrast Combinations

It's possible to create a page using all the principles discussed so far, yet still keep it relatively clean and attractive. The samples below and on the next page are proof.

This ad below uses size contrast (the tree graphic), value contrast (the gray type versus black type), and texture and shape contrast (the jagged, freeform tree shape in contrast to the ordered row of type and hairline rule).

OAKMEADOWS
C O N D O M I N I U M S

There are so many oaks at OakMeadows that we simply don't have room for all of them in this ad. So here are two or three of them just to give you the flavor. By the way, we also have some beautiful condominiums—if you can find them.

543-8334

Icons

Lenore Weiss

Poet and playwright Lenore Weiss has an M.A. in Creative Writing from San Francisco State University. She keeps up with the technological changes of her day as a desktop publisher of computer manuals, training materials and newsletters for the City of Oakland. Her creative writing focuses on how the current technology is transforming our use and conception of language. It "explores how the things that make us quiver the most can be expressed in that [technological] language." These poems were selected from a collection of 24 in a volume called *Icons*.

Icons
Lenore Weiss
1317 E. 27th Street
Oakland, CA 94604
(415) 261-7492 (evenings)
$5

I CRY OUT FOR LOVE

If there were an icon I could point to in my life,

I'd drag myself to the place and click,

See me rise from the bathtub squeaking clean, not a wife

Exactly, but imparted with several new tricks

How to juggle the monochrome needs of my soul mid-air;

But although I'd be a mouse to my own lion

Gnaw at these criss-crossed grids of hair,

Each time we return from counseling, I stop trying,

At point blank range I'm dead.

What is it that holds me back from touching you,

My heart's downloaded with Russian Roulette,

Whenever we try to talk it's ruination.

But if somehow I could find the icon on which to click,

And learn to forgive.

Plant blossoms outside your house

To tame the wild children of broken noses

Who come like hamsters nibbling at your doubt

In gigglebytes up the porch step wearing jumburritos

And cellophane candy wrappers, crinkling them;

French fry spears and play blood splatter,

There's the horn honk, who's a venture success

On the street where it's money and cars that matter.

Give them sweet bouquets as a childhood reminder

Not to grow up so quickly they forget

How a daisy is a love finder,

Or the honeysuckle a hummingbird's golden trumpet,

Or how, in encapsulated format, they are the seedlings

Of worldwide peace.

Moving On

This chapter has introduced several design principles and effects that can be used in creating a one-color document. The examples given so far, however, have mostly been in black and white. Using gray opens up an entirely new dimension. The following chapters investigate gray effects more closely; they also include many published examples of work by accomplished graphic designers working on personal computers.

Enjoy the visual feast!

The sample opposite has a light gray screened background (value contrast) and a large initial "L" and "I" adjacent to smaller body copy (size contrast). The single curve on the page, a "torn" block (texture contrast) with the headline reversed out of it, runs into the straight lines on the right side of the page (shape contrast); and the thin lines—repeated in the "Verbiage" logo (position contrast)—nicely balance the heavy "torn" block on the left (weight contrast). Well done!

2
Put It in Black and White

Color or even a lot of neat gray effects can sometimes cover up a poor design. But creating an interesting, lively design with black and white alone requires skill acquired through practice and experimentation.

This chapter serves as a sort of primer of black-and-white attention-getting elements. You may choose to use them as guides for your own designs. But remember that there are no hard-and-fast rules in graphic design. The design suggestions in this chapter are not meant to be followed blindly. After one has mastered the basics, the "rules" of graphic design can be broken.

Reverses

A reverse is an image, a graphic accent, or type that appears white (or the color of the paper) against a black or dark background. The subhead above, for instance, would be described as 11-point Helvetica bold *reversed out* of 50 percent gray. A reverse draws attention to the page by creating a value contrast.

(Right) All type on these black magazine covers is reversed. The words "GEM" and "magazine," set in Serif Gothic on all the covers, are quite readable. The 10-point type across from the graphic, however, varies in its readability. The upper left example is set in Optima Bold; the upper right in Bookman; and the lower left in Lucida Sans Bold. All three of these samples are more readable than the lines set in Bauer Bodoni at the lower right. Poor readability in faces with strong thick/thin contrast (like Bodoni) is even more evident in longer text blocks.

Although Bodoni is one of the worst faces for reversed type, at large point sizes it's not a problem. As a rule, when reversing, keep it large and bold.

Reverses add a significant amount of interest to an ordinary page of type. Here are more samples of this technique using just black and white.

As you work with reverses, be aware of the following pitfalls:

• *Avoid reversing out a large amount of text.* Our eyes and brains have been trained to read black type on a white page ever since our first kindergarten primer. A lot of white copy on a black background tires the eye. As blocks of reversed type get longer, chances increase that your text will be passed over.

• *Avoid reversing out a typeface with a dramatic thick/thin contrast in small point sizes.* Bodoni, Fenice, Broadway—these modern faces spell trouble when reversed out of black. The fine lines of these letterforms tend to fill in, especially if the printing job is less than perfect. If you must use a small point size, choose a medium or bold sans-serif face, or a serif face with even strokes like Bookman, Congress or Rockwell.

SERVING THE BALSA MODEL PLANE INDUSTRY   APRIL 1990

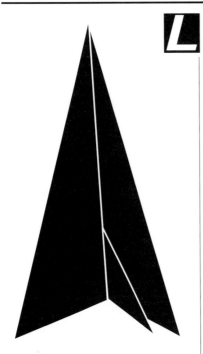

THE STEALTH MODEL is rapidly becoming the most popular in the industry.

Lorem ipsum dolor sit amet, consectetuer adipiscing elit, sed diam nonummy nibh euismod tincidunt ut laoreet dolore magna aliquam erat volutpat. Ut wisi enim ad minim veniam, quis nostrud exerci tation ullamcorper suscipit lobortis nisl ut aliquip ex ea commodo consequat. Duis autem vel eum iriure dolor in hendrerit in vulputate velit esse molestie consequat, vel illum dolore eu feugiat nulla facilisis at vero eros et accumsan et iusto odio dignissim qui blandit praesent luptatum zzril delenit augue duis dolore te feugait nulla facilisi. Lorem ipsum dolor sit amet, consectetuer adipiscing elit, sed diam nonummy nibh euismod tincidunt ut laoreet dolore magna aliquam erat volutpat. Ut wisi enim ad minim veniam, quis nostrud exerci tation ullamcorper suscipit lobortis nisl ut aliquip ex ea commodo consequat. Duis autem vel eum iriure dolor in hendrerit in vulputate velit esse molestie consequat, vel illum dolore eu feugiat nulla facilisis at vero eros et accumsan et iusto odio dignissim qui blandit praesent luptatum zzril delenit augue duis dolore te feugait nulla facilisi. Nam liber tempor cum soluta nobis eleifend option congue nihil imperdiet doming id quod mazim placerat facer possim assum. Lorem ipsum dolor sit amet, consectetuer adipiscing elit, sed diam nonummy nibh euismod tincidunt ut laoreet dolore magna aliquam erat volutpat.

This sample shows a newsletter nameplate reversed out of black, similar to the "Nightlife" headline at the beginning of Chapter 1. The difference here is that the descender, or the lower part, of the "g" has been left black, creating an eye-catching effect without losing readability. The subhead, set in a sans-serif face in all caps, is reversed out of a black bar about the same thickness as the strokes of the letters in the nameplate, creating a harmonious effect.

6

Lorem ipsum dolor sit amet, consectetuer adipiscing elit, sed diam nonummy nibh euismod tincidunt ut laoreet dolore magna aliquam erat volutpat. Ut wisi enim ad minim veniam, quis nostrud exerci tation ullamcorper suscipit lobortis nisl ut aliquip ex ea commodo consequat. Duis autem vel eum iriure dolor in hendrerit in vulputate velit esse molestie consequat, vel illum dolore eu feugiat nulla facilisis at vero eros et accumsan et iusto odio dignissim qui blandit praesent luptatum zzril delenit augue duis dolore te feugait nulla facilisi. Lorem ipsum dolor sit amet, consectetuer adipiscing elit, sed diam nonummy nibh euismod tincidunt ut laoreet dolore magna aliquam erat volutpat. Ut wisi enim ad minim veniam, quis nostrud exerci tation ullamcorper suscipit lobortis nisl ut aliquip ex ea commodo consequat.

Duis autem vel eum iriure dolor in hendrerit in vulputate velit esse molestie consequat, vel illum dolore eu feugiat nulla facilisis at vero eros et accumsan et iusto odio dignissim qui blandit praesent luptatum zzril delenit augue duis dolore te feugait nulla facilisi. Nam liber tempor cum soluta nobis eleifend option congue nihil imperdiet doming id quod mazim placerat facer possim assum. Lorem ipsum dolor sit amet, consectetuer adipiscing elit, sed diam nonummy nibh euismod tincidunt ut laoreet dolore magna aliquam erat volutpat. Ut wisi enim ad minim veniam, quis nostrud exerci tation ullamcorper suscipit lobortis nisl ut aliquip ex ea commodo consequat.

Duis autem vel eum iriure dolor in hendrerit in vulputate velit esse molestie consequat, vel illum dolore eu feugiat nulla facilisis at vero eros et accumsan et iusto odio dignissim qui blandit praesent luptatum zzril delenit augue duis dolore te feugait nulla facilisi. Lorem ipsum dolor sit amet, consectetuer adipiscing elit, sed diam nonummy nibh euismod tincidunt ut laoreet dolore magna aliquam erat volutpat. Duis autem vel eum iriure dolor in hendrerit in vulputate velit esse molestie consequat, vel illum dolore eu feugiat nulla facilisis at vero eros et accumsan et iusto odio dignissim qui blandit praesent luptatum zzril delenit augue duis dolore te feugait nulla facilisi.

Ut wisi enim ad minim veniam, quis nostrud exerci tation ullamcorper suscipit lobortis nisl ut aliquip ex ea commodo consequat. Duis autem vel eum iriure dolor in hendrerit in vulputate velit esse molestie consequat, vel illum dolore eu feugiat nulla facilisis at vero eros et accumsan et iusto odio dignissim qui blandit praesent luptatum zzril delenit augue duis dolore te feugait nulla facilisi.

Lorem ipsum dolor sit amet, consectetuer adipiscing elit, sed diam nonummy nibh euismod tincidunt ut laoreet dolore magna aliquam erat volutpat. Ut wisi enim ad minim veniam, quis nostrud exerci tation ullamcorper suscipit lobortis nisl ut aliquip ex ea commodo consequat. Duis autem vel eum iriure dolor in hendrerit in vulputate velit esse molestie consequat, vel illum dolore eu feugiat nulla facilisis at vero eros et accumsan et iusto odio dignissim qui blandit praesent luptatum zzril delenit augue duis dolore te feugait nulla facilisi. Nam liber tempor cum soluta nobis eleifend option congue nihil imperdiet doming id quod mazim placerat facer possim assum. Lorem ipsum dolor sit amet, consectetuer adipiscing elit, sed diam nonummy nibh euismod tincidunt ut laoreet dolore magna aliquam erat volutpat.

Ut wisi enim ad minim veniam, quis nostrud exerci tation ullamcorper suscipit lobortis nisl ut aliquip ex ea commodo consequat. Duis autem vel eum iriure dolor in hendrerit in vulputate velit esse molestie consequat, vel illum dolore eu feugiat nulla facilisis at vero eros et accumsan et iusto odio dignissim qui blandit praesent luptatum.

> **❝ I hated her and I loved her. That about sums it up, don't you think? Now get out of here. ❞**

Reversing a pull-quote out of a box is an excellent way to set it apart from the text. In this case, the box is an enlarged version of the one surrounding the folio (page number), creating a coordinated design.

CHAPTER 1

Tut wisi enim ad minim veniam, quis nostrud exerci tation ullamcorper suscipit lobortis nisl ut aliquip ex ea commodo consequat. Duis autem vel eum iriure dolor in hendrerit in vulputate velit esse molestie consequat, vel illum dolore eu feugiat nulla facilisis at vero eros et accumsan et iusto odio dignissim qui blandit praesent luptatum zzril delenit augue duis dolore te feugait nulla facilisi.

Ut wisi enim ad minim veniam, quis nostrud exerci tation ullamcorper suscipit lobortis nisl ut aliquip ex ea commodo consequat. Duis autem vel eum iriure dolor in hendrerit in vulputate velit esse molestie consequat, vel illum dolore eu feugiat nulla facilisis at vero eros et accumsan et iusto odio dignissim qui blandit praesent luptatum.

Letters, words and numbers can be reversed out of other letters, words and numbers. Although the two examples shown probably shouldn't be on the same page together (their combined effect is distracting rather than pleasant to look at), individually they are good examples of "internal reversals."

Initial Caps

Initial caps draw attention to the copy because of their size and blackness relative to the smaller text block they accompany. They can vary in size from only slightly larger than the text to huge, becoming the dominant element on the page. Keep in mind, though, that the larger the initial cap, the more attention it will get. So it's important to spend time choosing the individual letterforms. In general, one should either match the style of the initial cap to the text, or use a typeface that's in complete contrast to the text face. Remember that consistency is the best policy. Unless your publication is the latest underground art weekly, or a magazine in which each feature story has its own look and its own style of initial caps, it's best to stick to the same type face, size, weight and so on for all of your initial caps.

Use initial caps sparingly: usually one per column and not more than two per page. With double spreads (two pages side-by-side), take care that the caps don't spell an unintended word. Try to avoid "tombstoning"—that is, aligning the letters horizontally across the page. With the exception of the first initial cap in an article or text block, make sure initial caps aren't placed too close to the top or bottom of a page.

This was the noblest Roman of them all: all the conspirators, save only he, did that they did in envy of great Caesar; He only, in a general honest thought, and common good to all, made one of them.

The day may come when the rest of the animal creation may acquire those rights which never could have been witholden from them but by the hand of tyranny. The French have already discovered that the

WHAT I HAVE TO DO, I have to catch everybody if they start to go over the cliff—I mean if they're running and they don't look where they're going I have to come out from somewhere and catch them. That's all I'd do all day. I'd just be the catcher in the rye and all. I know it's crazy, but that's the only thing I'd really like to be.

RESOLUTE ARE YOU STILL, to win Odysseus' lady Penelope? Pit yourselves against the bow, and look among Akhaians for another's daughter. Gifts will be enough to court and take her. Let the best offer win.

(Opposite, top) This is an example of a *stick-up initial cap*. Note how the capital "T" has the text tucked close to its foot. Capitals "P" and "F" also should be treated this way.

(Opposite, second) This *hanging initial cap* sits to the side of the text block. Unlike most other kinds of initial caps that look best when bottom-aligned with a line from the text, hanging caps are more flexible and can be aligned with the text at the top or bottom of the letterform, or even somewhere in between.

(Opposite, third) *Drop caps* require the text to wrap around them. With angular letters like "W," "V" and "A," the text should follow the slope of the letterform. Another technique shown here that makes text more inviting to the reader is the use of all capitals for the first few words of the paragraph. If available, use true small caps for this purpose, because they blend more smoothly into the text.

(Opposite, bottom) Reverses can bring attention to both drop caps and hanging caps. This example also uses true small caps, that is, capital letters that measure slightly higher than a lowercase letter of the font, yet are almost as wide as a regular capital. Small caps blend into the text more readily than regular caps.

(Below) An example of an initial cap at work on a well-balanced page. The typeface for the drop cap is Machine, a heavy style that provides good contrast and balance with the strong black-and-white graphic at the bottom of the page.

OREM IPSUM DOLOR SIT amet, consectetuer adipiscing elit, sed diam nonummy nibh euismod tincidunt ut laoreet dolore magna aliquam erat volutpat. Ut wisi enim ad minim veniam, quis nostrud exerci tation ullamcorper suscipit lobortis nisl ut aliquip ex ea commodo consequat. Duis autem vel eum iriure dolor in hendrerit in vulputate velit esse molestie consequat, vel illum dolore eu feugiat nulla facilisis at vero eros et accumsan et iusto odio dignissim qui blandit praesent luptatum zzril delenit augue duis dolore te feugait nulla facilisi. Lorem ipsum dolor sit amet, consectetuer adipiscing elit, sed diam nonummy nibh euismod tincidunt ut laoreet dolore magna aliquam erat volutpat. Ut wisi enim ad minim veniam, quis nostrud exerci tation ullamcorper suscipit lobortis nisl ut aliquip ex ea commodo consequat.

tem vel eum iriure dolor in hendrerit in vulputate velit esse molestie consequat, vel illum dolore eu feugiat nulla facilisis at vero eros et accumsan et iusto odio dignissim qui blandit praesent luptatum zzril delenit augue duis dolore te feug

Shadows

Shades of gray can contribute a great deal to the success of shadows and shadowed type (see Chapter 3 for more examples). But creating shadows with black and white alone is worth exploring.

The purpose of the shadow is to lend a three-dimensional effect to the flat page, and to draw the reader's attention to that area. A few programs for the computer offer automatic drop shadows, so the technique has become overused. Still, variations of the standard drop shadow like the ones pictured here are sufficiently interesting to be used occasionally.

(Below) This attempt at a black drop shadow for a white initial cap is not particularly successful. Although the "G" is large, it's not very readable.
A better solution is a gray shadow for black type. (Complete black/gray/white shadow combinations are explored in the next chapter.)

atsby's noteriety, spread about by the hundreds who had accepted his hospitality and so become authorities upon his past, had increased all summer until he fell just short of being news.

atsby's noteriety, spread about by the hundreds who had accepted his hospitality and so become authorities upon his past, had increased all summer until he fell just short of being news.

The drop shadows below show a few of the shadow effects that can be created with black and white.

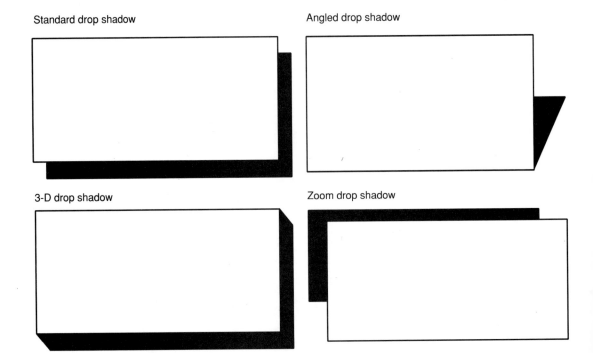

Standard drop shadow

Angled drop shadow

3-D drop shadow

Zoom drop shadow

PROGRESS REPORT

Lorem ipsum dolor sit amet, consectetuer adipiscing elit, sed diam nonummy nibh euismod tincidunt ut laoreet dolore magna aliquam erat volutpat. Ut wisi enim ad minim veniam, quis nostrud exerci tation ullamcorper suscipit lobortis nisl ut aliquip ex ea commodo consequat. Duis autem vel eum iriure dolor in hendrerit in vulputate velit esse molestie consequat, vel illum dolore eu feugiat nulla facilisis at vero eros et accumsan et iusto odio dignissim qui blandit praesent luptatum zzril delenit augue duis dolore te feugait nulla facilisi. Lorem ipsum dolor sit amet, consectetuer adipiscing elit, sed diam nonummy nibh euismod tincidunt ut laoreet dolore magna aliquam erat volutpat. Ut wisi enim ad minim veniam, quis nostrud exerci tation ullamcorper suscipit lobortis nisl ut aliquip ex ea commodo consequat.

Duis autem vel eum iriure dolor in hendrerit in vulputate velit esse molestie consequat, vel illum dolore eu feugiat nulla facilisis at vero eros et accumsan et iusto odio dignissim qui blandit praesent luptatum zzril delenit augue duis dolore te feugait nulla facilisi. Nam liber tempor cum soluta nobis eleifend option congue nihil imperdiet doming id quod mazim placerat facer possim assum. Lorem ipsum dolor sit amet, consectetuer adipiscing elit, sed diam nonummy nibh euismod tincidunt ut laoreet dolore magna

commodo consequat. Duis autem vel eum iriure dolor in hendrerit in vulputate velit esse molestie consequat, vel illum dolore eu feugiat nulla facilisis at vero eros et accumsan et iusto odio dignissim qui blandit praesent luptatum zzril delenit augue duis dolore te feugait nulla facilisi. Lorem ipsum dolor sit amet, consectetuer adipiscing elit, sed diam nonummy nibh euismod tincidunt ut laoreet dolore magna aliquam erat volutpat. Ut wisi enim ad minim veniam, quis nostrud exerci tation ullamcorper suscipit lobortis nisl ut aliquip ex ea commodo consequat.

Duis autem vel eum iriure dolor in hendrerit in vulputate velit esse molestie consequat, vel illum dolore eu feugiat nulla facilisis at vero eros et accumsan et iusto odio dignissim qui blandit praesent luptatum zzril delenit augue

aliquam erat volutpat. Ut wisi enim ad minim veniam, quis nostrud exerci tation ullamcorper suscipit lobortis nisl ut aliquip ex ea commodo consequat. Duis autem vel eum iriure dolor in hendrerit in vulputate velit esse molestie consequat, vel illum dolore eu feugiat nulla facilisis at vero eros et accumsan et iusto odio dignissim qui blandit praesent luptatum zzril delenit augue duis dolore te feugait nulla facilisi. Lorem ipsum dolor sit amet, consectetuer adipiscing elit, sed diam nonummy nibh euismod tincidunt ut laoreet dolore magna aliquam erat volutpat.

Ut wisi enim ad minim veniam, quis nostrud exerci tation ullamcorper suscipit lobortis nisl ut aliquip ex ea commodo consequat. Duis autem vel eum iriure dolor in hendrerit in vulputate velit esse molestie consequat, vel illum dolore eu feugiat nulla facilisis at vero eros et accumsan et iusto odio dignissim qui blandit praesent luptatum zzril delenit augue duis dolore te feugait

nulla facilisi. Lorem ipsum dolor sit amet, consectetuer adipiscing elit, sed diam nonummy nibh euismod tincidunt ut laoreet dolore magna aliquam erat volutpat. Ut wisi enim ad minim veniam, quis nostrud exerci tation ullamcorper suscipit lobortis nisl ut aliquip ex ea commodo consequat. Duis autem vel eum iriure dolor in hendrerit in vulputate velit esse molestie consequat, vel illum dolore eu feugiat nulla facilisis at vero eros et accumsan et iusto odio dignissim qui blandit praesent luptatum zzril delenit augue duis dolore te feugait nulla facilisi.

Lorem ipsum dolor sit amet, consectetuer adipiscing elit, sed diam nonummy nibh euismod tincidunt ut laoreet dolore magna aliquam erat volutpat. Ut wisi enim ad minim veniam, quis nostrud exerci tation ullamcorper suscipit lobortis nisl ut aliquip ex ea commodo consequat. Duis autem vel eum iriure dolor in hendrerit in vulputate velit esse

dolore eu feugiat nulla facilisis at vero eros et accumsan et iusto odio dignissim qui blandit praesent luptatum zzril delenit augue duis dolore te feugait nulla facilisi. Lorem ipsum dolor sit amet, consectetuer adipiscing elit, sed

An example of a drop shadow as it sits on the page. Note how the white area with type appears to be in front of the shadow. Also notice that the white area is not bound by a rule at the top and left side— a technique that gives the page a more spacious feeling.

Rules and Borders

Rules and borders are great ways to enliven your layout. They can be effectively used to organize material on the page, frame or underscore important text, or as an overall design element.

Rules placed under type should be used with caution. In typewritten copy, an underscore is the substitute for the more elegant tools of emphasis (such as bold and italic type) available for typeset copy. So an effort should be made to keep rules from looking like "underlining."

(Left) This assortment of rules and borders is available in a typical page layout program.

(Right) Here are a few of the various rule weights in use.

90NEWS

PROGRESS REPORT

Lorem ipsum dolor sit amet, consectetuer adipiscing elit, sed diam nonummy nibh euismod tincidunt ut laoreet dolore magna aliquam erat volutpat. Ut wisi enim ad minim veniam, quis nostrud exerci tation ullamcorper suscipit loabortis nisl ut aliquip ex ea commodo consequat. Duis te feugait nulla facilisi. Lorem ipsum dolor sit amet, consectetuer adipiscing elit, nibh euismod.

Ut wisi enim ad minim veniam, quis nostrud exerci tation ullamcorper suscipit lobortis nisl ut aliquip ex ea commodo consequat. Duis autem vel eum iriure dolor in hendrerit in vulputate velit esse molestie consequat, vel illum dolore eu feugiat nulla facilisis at vero eros et accumsan et iusto odio dignissim qui blandit praesent luptatum zzril delenit augue duis dolore te feugait nulla facilisi. Lorem ipsum dolor sit amet, consectetuer adipiscing elit, sed diam nonummy nibh euismod tincidunt ut laoreet dolore magna aliquam erat volutpat. Ut wisi enim ad minim veniam, quis nostrud exerci tation ullamcorper suscipit lobortis nisl ut aliquip ex ea commodo consequat. Duis autem vel iriure dolor in hendrerit in vulputate velit esse molestie consequat, vel illum dolore eu feugiat nulla facilisis at vero ero delenit augue duis dolore te feugait nulla facilisi.

Consectetuer adipiscing elit, sed diam nonummy nibh euismod tincidunt ut laoreet dolore magna aliquam erat volutpat. Ut wisi enim ad minim veniam, quis nostrud exerci tation ullamcorper suscipit lobortis nisl ut aliquip ex consequat. Duis autem vel eum iriure dolor velit esse molestie consequat, vel illum dolore eu feugiat nulla odio dignissim qui blandit praesent luptatum zzril delim ad minim veniam, quis nostrud exerci tation ullamcorper suscipit lobortis nisl ut aliquip ex ea commodo consequat. Duis te feugait nulla facilisi. Lorem ipsum dolor sit amet, consectetuer adipiscing elit, sed diam nonummy nibh euismod tincidunt ut laoreet dolore magna aliquam erat volutpat.

Ut wisi enim ad minim veniam, im ad minim veniam, quis nostrud exerci tation ullamcorper suscipit lobortis nisl ut aliquip ex ea commodo consequat. Duis te feugait nulla facilisi. Lorem ipsum dolor sit amet, consectetuer adipiscing elit, sed diam nonummy nibh euismod tincidunt ut laoreet ullamcorper suscipit lobortis nisl ut aliquip ex ea commodo consequat. Duis autem vel eum iriure dolim ad minim veniam, quis nostrud exerci tation ullamcorper suscipit lobortis nisl ut aliquip ex ea commodo consequat. Duis te feugait nulla facilisi. Lorem ipsum dolor sit amet, consectetuer adipiscing elit, sed diam nonummy nibh

euismod tincidunt ut laoreet dolore magna aliquam erat volutpat.

Ut wisi enim ad minim veniam, quis nostrud exerci tation ullamcorper suscipit lobortis nisl ut aliquip ex ea commodo consequat. Duis autem vel eum iriure dolor in hendrerit in vulputate velit esse molestie consequat, vel illum dolore eu feugiat nulla facilisis at vero eros et accumsan et iusto odio dignissim qui blandit praesent luptatum zzril delenit augue duis dolore te feugait nulla facili. Lorem ipsum dolor sit amet, consectetuer adipiscing elit, sed diam nonummy nibh euismod tincior in hendrerit in vulputate velit esse molestie consequat, vel illum dolore eu feugiat nulla facilisis at vero eros et accumsan et iusto odio dignissim qui blandit praesent luptatum zzril delenit augue duis dolore te feugait nulla facili. Lorem ipsum dolor sit amet, consectetuer adipiscing elit, sed diam nonummy nibh euismod tincium dolore eu feugiat nulla facilisis at vero

Eros et accumsan et iusto odio dignissim qui blandit praesent luptatum zzril delenit augue duis dolore te feugait nulla facilisi. Lorem ipsum dolor sit amet, consectetuer adipiscing elit, sed diam nonummy nibh euismod tincienit augue duis dolore te feugait nulla facilisi. Lorem ipsum dolor sit amet, consectetuer adipiscing e te feugait nulla facilisi. Nam liber tempor

A rule can add a nice touch to a headline. It should not overpower the type, nor should it dwindle to insignificance. In this example, the rounded line endings of the underscores match nicely with the soft endings of the italic letterforms. The border's weight and rounded corners match the title's underscore.

R A T E   C A R D

SIZE	WEEKDAY	WEEKEND
Full page	$2400.00	$2750.00
Half page	1400.00	1600.00
Third Page	1000.00	1175.00
Quarter page	750.00	850.00
Sixth page	500.00	500.00
Eighth page	400.00	485.00
Tenth page	300.00	370.00
Column inch	45.00	55.00

The rules for this rate card act as a guide for the eye, making it easy to find the cost for the various ad sizes. They also dress up the document in a stylish, modern way—a good example of repetition for effect.

C O M M E N T A R Y

Lorem ipsum dolor sit amet, consectetuer adipiscing elit, sed diam nonummy nibh euismod tincidunt ut laoreet dolore magna aliquam erat volutpat. Ut wisi enim ad minim veniam, quis nostrud exerci tation ullamcorper suscipit lobortis nisl ut aliquip ex ea commodo consequat. Duis autem vel eum iriure dolor in hendrerit in vulputate velit esse molestie consequat, vel illum dolore eu feugiat nulla facilisis at vero eros et accumsan et iusto odio dignissim qui blandit praesent luptatum zzril delenit augue duis dolore te feugait nulla facilisi. Lorem ipsum dolor sit amet, consectetuer adipiscing elit, sed diam nonummy nibh euismod tincidunt ut laoreet dolore magna aliquam erat volutpat. Ut wisi enim ad minim veniam, quis nostrud exerci tation ullamcorper suscipit lobortis nisl ut aliquip ex ea commodo consequat.

Duis autem vel eum iriure dolor in hendrerit in vulputate velit esse molestie consequat, vel illum dolore eu feugiat nulla facilisis at vero eros et accumsan et iusto odio dignissim qui blandit praesent luptatum zzril delenit augue duis dolore te feugait nulla facilisi. Nam liber tempor cum soluta nobis eleifend option congue nihil imperdiet doming id quod mazim placerat facer possim assum. Lorem ipsum dolor sit amet, consectetuer adipiscing elit, sed diam nonummy nibh euismod tincidunt ut laoreet dolore magna aliquam erat volutpat. Ut wisi enim ad minim veniam, quis nostrud exerci tation ullamcorper suscipit lobortis nisl ut aliquip ex ea commodo consequat.

Lorem ipsum dolor sit amet, consectetuer adipiscing elit, sed diam nonummy nibh euismod tincidunt ut laoreet dolore magna aliquam erat volutpat. Ut wisi enim ad minim veniam, quis nostrud exerci tation ullamcorper suscipit lobortis nisl ut aliquip ex ea commodo consequat. Duis autem vel eum iriure dolor in hendrerit in vulputate velit esse molestie consequat, vel illum dolore.

Work became a prison.
Years ago, the father wielded
a pick-axe; today, the son
pounded computer keys.

Lorem ipsum dolor sit amet, consectetuer adipiscing elit, sed diam nonummy nibh euismod tincidunt ut laoreet dolore magna aliquam erat volutpat. Ut wisi enim ad minim veniam, quis nostrud exerci tation ullamcorper suscipit lobortis nisl ut aliquip ex ea commodo consequat. Duis autem vel eum iriure dolor in hendrerit in vulputate velit esse molestie consequat, vel illum dolore. Lorem ipsum dolor sit amet, consectetuer adipiscing elit, sed diam nonummy nibh euismod tincidunt ut laoreet dolore magna aliquam erat volutpat. Ut wisi enim ad minim veniam, quis nostrud exerci tation ullamcorper suscipit lobortis nisl ut aliquip.

Duis autem vel eum iriure dolor in hendrerit in vulputate velit esse molestie consequat, vel illum dolore eu feugiat nulla facilisis at vero eros et accumsan et iusto odio dignissim qui blandit praesent luptatum zzril delenit augue duis dolore te feugait nulla facilisi. Lorem ipsum dolor sit amet, consectetuer adipiscing elit, sed diam nonummy nibh euismod tincidunt ut laoreet dolore magna aliquam erat volutpat. Lorem ipsum dolor sit amet, consectetuer adipiscing elit, sed diam nonummy nibh euismod tincidunt ut laoreet dolore magna aliquam erat volutpat. ■

Here rules are used as a design element, drawing the eye to the section heading and setting off the pull-quote in an interesting manner. Note also the rules between the lines of the pull-quote.

These decorative borders are taken from a clip art collection. With a little time, patience and creativity, you can create your own in a drawing program. When applying the border to a page layout, make the border match the theme of the text (for example, a Roman border for a story about Pompeii).

(Opposite) This Art Deco border was taken from a clip art collection and modified to create the cover for a book jacket.

The Classic Commentary on H.P. Blavatsky's
Secret Doctrine, elucidating the universal principles
of the Wisdom Tradition

FUNDAMENTALS OF THE
ESOTERIC
PHILOSOPHY
GOTTFRIED DE PURUCKER

Bleeds

Bleeds refer to extra areas of ink coverage that extend beyond the *trim* or *live matter area* of the page (not to be confused with ink that 'bleeds" or runs on cheap paper). To bleed an element means to print it to the edge of the paper. You can bleed rules and borders, large letterforms, photos, large solid areas and other elements. A bleed gives the page a feeling of expansiveness; the page seems larger than it actually is, unbounded by margins.

In some cases, bleeds may be more trouble than they're worth. For example, if you want to bleed a scanned image—a photo—off the side of an 8 ½ x 11 inch newsletter the first problem occurs when you want to proof your design on your laser printer.

Since most printers leave a margin of ¼ to ⅛ of an inch on a letter-sized sheet, you'll need to either tile the page (print it in sections) and manually cut and paste the pieces together, or print the page smaller than full size and trim off the margins, creating a scaled-down preview of how the bleed will look on the finished piece. Unless you can learn to visualize the result from a standard laser proof, a bleed can end up taking a lot of time.

If you use bleeds, plan on spending a little more money when you take your camera-ready art to your commercial printer. There may be an extra paper charge if the printer needs to cut paper to size for your job. When the printing is completed, the paper will need to be cut again—this time to the trim size.

In this example of a simple bleed, two pairs of rules run off the left side of the page.

210

Treatment of Unruly Children

Lorem ipsum dolor sit amet, consectetuer adipiscing elit, sed diam nonummy nibh euismod tincidunt ut laoreet dolore magna aliquam erat volutpat. Ut wisi enim ad minim veniam, quis nostrud exerci tation ullamcorper suscipit lobortis nisl ut aliquip ex ea commodo consequat. Duis autem vel eum iriure dolor in hendrerit in vulputate velit esse molestie consequat, vel illum dolore eu feugiat nulla facilisis at vero eros et accumsan et iusto odio dignissim qui blandit praesent luptatum zzril delenit augue duis dolore te feugait nulla facilisi. Lorem ipsum dolor sit amet, consectetuer adipiscing elit, sed diam nonummy nibh euismod tincidunt ut laoreet dolore magna aliquam erat volutpat.

Ut wisi enim ad minim veniam, quis nostrud exerci tation ullamcorper suscipit lobortis nisl ut aliquip ex ea commodo consequat. Duis autem vel eum iriure dolor in hendrerit in vulputate velit esse molestie consequat, vel illum dolore eu feugiat nulla facilisis at vero eros et accumsan et iusto odio dignissim qui blandit praesent luptatum zzril delenit augue duis dolore te feugait nulla facilisi.

Treatment of Incompetent Parents

Duis autem vel eum iriure dolor in hendrerit in vulputate velit esse molestie consequat, vel illum dolore eu feugiat nulla facilisis at vero eros et accumsan et iusto odio dignissim qui blandit praesent luptatum zzril delenit augue duis dolore te feugait nulla facilisi. Lorem ipsum dolor sit amet, consectetuer adipiscing elit, sed diam nonummy nibh euismod tincidunt ut laoreet dolore magna aliquam erat volutpat. Ut wisi enim ad minim veniam, quis nostrud exerci tation ullamcorper suscipit lobortis nisl ut aliquip ex ea commodo consequat.

The "M" in this menu
bleeds on two sides, the
top and left. Note how this
bleed makes the page
appear slightly larger. Also
notice the effective use of
size contrast.

TREEHOUSE RESTAURANT

An American in Paris

Lorem ipsum dolor sit amet, consectetuer adipiscing elit, sed diam nonummy nibh euismod tincidunt ut laoreet dolore magna aliquam erat volutpat. Ut wisi enim ad minim veniam, quis nostrud exerci tation ullamcorper suscipit lobortis nisl ut aliquip ex ea commodo consequat. Duis autem vel eum iriure dolor in hendrerit in vulputate velit esse molestie consequat, vel illum dolore eu feugiat nulla facilisis at vero eros et accumsan et iusto odio dignissim qui blandit praesent luptatum zzril delenit augue duis dolore te feugait nulla facilisi. Lorem ipsum dolor sit amet, consectetuer adipiscing elit, sed diam nonummy nibh euismod tincidunt ut laoreet dolore magna aliquam erat volutpat. Ut wisi enim ad minim veniam, quis nostrud exerci tation ullamcorper suscipit lobortis nisl ut aliquip ex ea commodo consequat.

(Above) This book page bleeds on three sides (similar to *The Gray Book's* chapter openings) and is an effective repetitive theme for any long publication.

(Left) Although the graphic for this brochure cover appears to bleed on three sides, it actually only bleeds off the top and right. Assuming that the brochure opens to the left, the lower left point of the star actually wraps around to the back panel.

(Below) For this book
cover that bleeds on
all four sides, your
commercial printer would
need to know that the job
entailed "heavy coverage,"
since a lot of ink would be
required to run it.

Rotated Elements

Unless your publication is "artsy" or whimsical, it's best to exercise caution when using rotated elements. Although they add interest, that benefit is often outweighed by a loss in readability.

Elements rotated so the right side is higher than the left are considered more positively oriented. This is especially true with rotated type.

This magazine cover walks a fine line between good design and poor readability. The layout is very strong, yet the teaser lines—highlighting the articles inside—are difficult to read because of their angle. If the teaser lines were placed as expected with no angle, the design would suffer. In this case, the art director got a "go-ahead" from the editor to use the sample shown because of the impact of the striking design.

(Below) In this example, the rotated graphic images are essential in making an attractive page design. Without them the layout, dominated by rows of horizontal type and rules, would have been rather monotonous.

(Below) Again, the rotated elements add a touch of interest to the page. Although each pull-quote has two full sentences and is reversed out of black, readability does not suffer. The type is large, legible and rotated only a few degrees.

Lorem ipsum dolor sit amet, consectetuer adipiscing elit, sed diam

nonummy nibh euismod tincidunt ut laoree

aliquam erat volutpat. Ut wisi enim ad min

nostrud exerci tation ullamcorper suscipit lobort...

ea commodo consequat. Duis autem vel eum iriure dolor in

ltate velit esse molestie consequat, vel illum

lla facilisis at vero eros et accumsan et iusto

landit praesent luptatum zzril delenit augue

duis dolore te feugait nulla facilisi. Lorem ipsum dolor sit amet,

consectetuer adipiscing elit, sed diam nonummy nibh euismod

tincidunt ut laoreet dolore magna aliquam erat volutpat. Ut wisi

enim ad minim veniam, quis nostrud exerci tation ullamcorper

suscipit lobortis nisl ut aliquip ex ea commodo consequat.

Duis autem vel eum iriure dolor in ...ate velit esse

molestie consequat, vel illum ...ulla facilisis at

vero eros et accumsan.

Duis autem vel eum iriure dolor in hendrerit in vulputate velit esse molestie consequat, vel illum dolore eu feugiat nulla facilisis at vero eros et iusto odio dignissim qui blandit praesent luptatum zzril delenit augue duis dolore te feugait nulla facilisi. Lorem ipsum dolor sit amet, consectetuer adipiscing elit, sed diam nonummy nibh euismod tincidunt ut laoreet dolore magna aliquam erat volutpat.

Randy Dillon was a shark. If you wanted to play with the sharks, you couldn't be a tuna.

Lorem ipsum dolor sit amet, consectetuer adipiscing elit, sed diam nonummy nibh euismod tincidunt ut laoreet dolore magna aliquam erat volutpat. Ut wisi enim ad minim veniam, quis nostrud exerci tation ullamcorper suscipit nisl ut aliquip ex ea commodo consequat. Duis autem vel eum iriure dolor in hendrerit in vulputate velit esse molestie consequat, vel illum dolore eu feugiat nulla facilisis at vero eros et accumsan et iusto odio dignissim qui blandit praesent luptatum zzril delenit augue duis dolore te feugait nulla facilisi. Lorem ipsum dolor sit amet, consectetuer adipiscing elit, sed diam nonummy nibh euismod tincidunt ut laoreet dolore magna aliquam erat volutpat. Ut wisi enim ad minim veniam, quis nostrud exerci tation ullamcorper suscipit lobortis nisl ut aliquip ex ea commodo consequat.

Duis autem vel eum iriure dolor in hendrerit in vulputate velit esse molestie consequat, vel illum dolore eu feugiat nulla facilisis at vero eros et accumsan et iusto odio dignissim qui blandit praesent luptatum zzril delenit augue duis dolore te feugait nulla facilisi. Nam liber tempor cum soluta nobis eleifend option congue nihil imperdiet doming id quod mazim placerat facer possim assum. Lorem ipsum dolor sit amet, consectetuer adipiscing elit, sed diam nonummy nibh euismod tincidunt ut laoreet dolore magna aliquam erat volutpat. Ut wisi enim ad minim veniam, quis nostrud exerci tation ullamcorper suscipit lobortis nisl ut aliquip ex ea commodo consequat.

Lorem ipsum dolor sit amet, consectetuer adipiscing elit, sed diam nonummy nibh euismod tincidunt ut laoreet dolore magna aliquam erat volutpat. Ut wisi enim ad minim veniam, quis nostrud exerci tation ullamcorper suscipit nisl ut aliquip ex ea commodo consequat. Duis autem vel eum iriure dolor in hendrerit in vulputate velit esse molestie consequat, vel illum dolore eu feugiat nulla facilisis at vero eros et accumsan et iusto odio dignissim qui blandit praesent luptatum zzril delenit augue duis dolore te feugait nulla facilisi. Lorem ipsum dolor sit amet, consectetuer adipiscing elit, sed diam nonummy nibh euismod tincidunt ut laoreet dolore magna aliquam erat volutpat.

"Randy was just different," said an old school chum. "We called him 'Fishface'."

Duis autem vel eum iriure dolor in hendrerit in vulputate velit esse molestie consequat, vel illum dolore eu feugiat nulla facilisis at vero eros et accumsan et iusto odio dignissim qui blandit praesent luptatum zzril delenit augue duis dolore te feugait nulla facilisi.

Patterns

Creative use of patterns can make a memorable impression on your reader. Here are a few samples of striking black-and-white patterns.

The Wine Taster's Guild

(Right) Type can be effectively used as a pattern. Some drawing programs let you "paste inside" a particular shape. Here the shape of a wine glass is formed by the words commonly used to describe wines.

(Right) On this report cover, the company logo was used to form the pattern, creating a *real* corporate look—an illusion of a large building with many windows. Looking at this simple arrangement of black on white, the eye completes the shapes of the windows and their overhangs.

Tower
Industries

(Below) This report cover
shows effective use of
"pattern-breaking." The
eye goes directly to the
type that has replaced the
triangles.

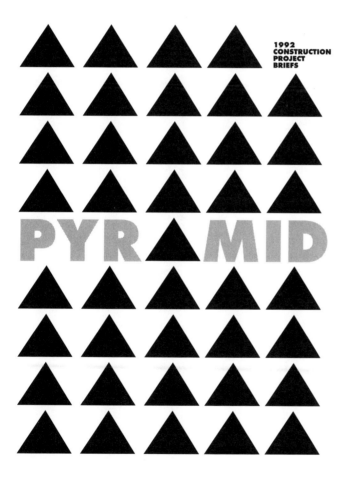

1992
CONSTRUCTION
PROJECT
BRIEFS

PYR▲MID

High-Contrast Scans

Black-and-white scanned images are referred to as one-bit images because the information needed to define each dot, or *pixel*, in the image can be stored as a single "on" (black) or "off" (white) signal. Such scanned images are often overlooked as a way to add interest to a page without adding shades of gray. Coarse scanned images and paint-type graphics (72 dpi) have fallen out of use because they appear rough compared to higher resolution (300 dpi and up) scans and to images created in a drawing or illustration program. Creating a high-contrast, or *posterized*, version of a scan of any resolution, however, brings out the essential features of the image. The development of autotrace features in many programs allows you to make smooth curves out of the rougher bit-mapped ones. Finally, thousands of one-bit black- and-white clip art images are available to help you enhance your document.

(Below) Autotracing the scanned tree image gives it a rough, artistic look, appropriate for the wintery feel of this business card. The calligraphy was also autotraced and "cleaned up" in an illustration program.

(Bottom) This magazine spread puts to good use a dynamic, high-contrast scanned image. A regular photo wouldn't pack the same punch.

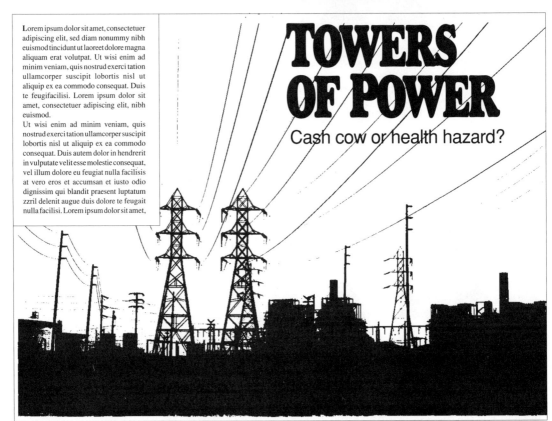

Lorem ipsum dolor sit amet, consectetuer adipiscing elit, sed diam nonummy nibh euismod tincidunt ut laoreet dolore magna aliquam erat volutpat. Ut wisi enim ad minim veniam, quis nostrud exerci tation ullamcorper suscipit lobortis nisl ut aliquip ex ea commodo consequat. Duis te feugifacilisi. Lorem ipsum dolor sit amet, consectetuer adipiscing elit, nibh euismod.

Ut wisi enim ad minim veniam, quis nostrud exerci tation ullamcorper suscipit lobortis nisl ut aliquip ex ea commodo consequat. Duis autem dolor in hendrerit in vulputate velit esse molestie consequat, vel illum dolore eu feugiat nulla facilisis at vero eros et accumsan et iusto odio dignissim qui blandit praesent luptatum zzril delenit augue duis dolore te feugait nulla facilisi. Lorem ipsum dolor sit amet,

FLYING DISK MONTHLY

How to play the wind

The NEGATIVE aspects of judging

(Left) Sometimes a negative image can be a great attention-getter, like this scan of a frisbee player. The use of such an unusual image is probably appropriate only because the teaser on the cover uses the word "negative"; otherwise, a regular scanned image would be more appropriate.

THE VERBUM INTERVIEW

Todd Rundgren, rock star, programmer and colorful presence at Macintosh developer events during the past few years, has been actively writing code — Hypercode, that is. (For those who worry that Todd has given up on music, he has a new solo album out. No synthesizers — no fooling. And he is still actively producing other bands.) He recently teamed up with programmer David Levine to found Utopia Grokware, a software development firm. Levine is an art school graduate and computer systems engineer who has worked in the games division of LucasFilm for the past five years. His Mac II screen saver, FlowFazer, is Utopia's first product.

Rundgren and Levine are enthusiastic visionaries. "Virtual reality" is a concept central to their approach to software development. "Cyberspace" is another central concept, the transcendent computing experience that will come from organically conceived, platform-independent software and more sophisticated I/O devices.

Verbum interviewed Todd and David at Utopia headquarters (the Rundgren residence) in Sausalito about the future evolution of computers, music as communication, and their own Hypercode software development.

Verbum: We've seen computing power come down from the mainframe to the mini and then to the micro, and we've seen the use of that power spread to the student, the musician, the artist. The intuitive interface, and the creative applications that allow people to express themselves, telecommunicate with others, publish and so on. Where are we going?

Todd Rundgren: Computers give people a chance to build alternative kinds of reality. And the interesting thing for bringing about major changes in the world — the advance of peace, for example — is that once we start to build realities, we start to question the purpose of our existence, because these invented realities can supplant the normal physical activities that people do with the activities that are representationally the same but don't involve the transfer of matter from one place to another, for example. Having that ability makes people realize how much of life is actually contained inside themselves. It's not

really out there but in here. And, once people start to realize that, they may realize the degree of control and power they have. They may stop just going around and being subjected to what happens — being subjected to outside forces all the time. That really it is a result of attitude. Now each of us will have the option of building our own virtual world inside the computer, the opportunity to create something completely. You've never had this option before, so maybe you've never even thought about the responsibility: "If I was God, what kind of world would I build?" Most people never get to that point. And it takes getting to that point personally for people to realize that within their own awareness, they *are* playing God. And they are either playing a pitiful victimized God, or they are playing a God who is aware and in control and informed.

Verbum: When you talk about creating

On music, component software and Utopia

realities with the computer, you're talking about hypermedia?

TR: In a certain sense. It's called hyper-this and hyper-that. But it's just a logical extension, a natural process. Nature will only allow certain things to survive and breathe, you know. Well, one of the things Nature is determined to kill off is the command line, the A prompt. Essentially, Nature has decided that the A prompt is just a lower life form that is eventually going to disappear.

Verbum: Yes. But hypermedia seems to me to be more than just doing away with the A prompt. There is something to be said for this ability to access information with a computer, to be able to learn, to

navigate. I'm very excited about the possibilities.

TR: The entire evolution of computers is an attempt to map the way people think into this external medium. And we start to think that there are rules about the kind of world that you're allowed to create in this medium — because there *are* certain rules in this medium, the A prompt being one of them. You know, everyone has a right to create a world that conforms exactly to what he or she wants, as long as the same freedom is extended to everybody else. This is a great opportunity to get all these maniacs with guns off the street, you know. Just plug 'em in and let them blast their brains out.

David Levine: The development of computers can be seen as highly idealistic. It's a nice ideal. You can look at life as a mass hallucination anyway, which is sort of extending and advancing the sophistication of physical medium, of our parent's imagined physical medium. In times past certain subsections of our civilization may have known or had scientific knowledge of communication — say, some sort of telepathic way of being able to instill common visualizations of some imagined reality in a group of people. But if that existed, it's been lost, and we don't know

Keep in mind that high-contrast images work well with layouts or products with a "hard edge," but would hardly be appropriate for a double-page spread on food, for instance.

As we've seen in previous pages, black and white doesn't need to be boring. Careful use of these two tones alone can provide a more effective, dramatic solution than using gray or additional color.

(Left) A high-contrast, rotated image with type serves as a focal point for the page. The black-and-white image works well here; a gray-scale image would have been fussier and carried less impact.

(Below) A simple black-and-white graphic serves as an appropriately stark image for this book jacket.

3
Playing With Gray

To most of the world, the word *gray* means "boring." Not so for designers limited to one-color work. For them, gray means "unlimited possibilities." The potential to design truly stunning gray-tinted layouts walks hand-in-hand with the possibility of creating an occasional design blunder. The purpose of this chapter is to guide you toward the former and away from the latter.

The following design effects are similar to those covered in the previous chapter on black and white, with the addition of shades of gray.

Imagine yourself a chef who has been offered a wide range of spices you never used before. Those spices are shades of gray, and this is the cookbook that will get you started. May your own recipes someday surpass those written here!

Before exploring the design potential of grays, it's important to understand the role *screens* play.

Screens

Gray shades are most commonly formed by *screening* black; the computer creates an apparent gray color by turning solid black into geometrically arranged black dots. The procedure is called screening because traditional graphic arts cameras use a screen between the black object and the film. This screen causes a dot pattern of the black object to be created on the exposed film.

If the gray is darker, the percentage of black is higher—let's say 80 or 90 percent. The black dots are large and the eye perceives a dark gray. If the percentage is low—10 to 20 percent—the dot is small and the eye sees a light gray.

Two considerations must be kept in mind when outputting and printing screens:

• *Screens look best output on film (negative) at 2540 dpi.* Although there are times when your options are limited and you must print at a lower resolution, the hi-res option gives the most accurate dot and the smoothest screen, especially with the gradient grays (see pages 76-79). When you output to negative, the printer can make printing plates directly from that output, giving you results that closely match what you want. If you output a positive, the quality is compromised through the processes because the printer must create a negative before making plates.

• *Your printed screens won't necessarily match what comes out of the imagesetter.* The lithographic printing process has a quirk called *dot gain*, a phenomenon that causes screened areas to look darker once they've been printed.

The circular insets on these samples are enlargements of the dot density and therefore the gray shade of their respective rectangles. The top sample is a 20 percent screen of black; the lower one is 80 percent.

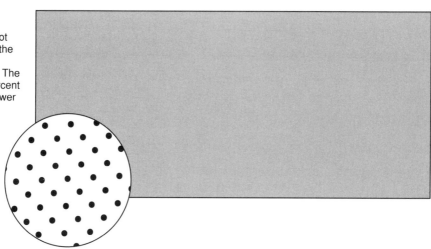

To compensate for dot gain, reduce the screen percentage on your computer by 10 to 30 percent, depending on paper stock (textured, uncoated stocks require greater reduction than glossy paper). For instance, if you want a finished product to match a 70 percent gray tone, create it at 50 percent on your computer.

At 20 percent and under, however, the phenomenon reverses: the printing press starts to ignore the dots, resulting in a kind of dot loss; and a 20 percent screened area output from the computer will look like 10 percent when printed.

Screening Type Using screens on type to get more "color" in a layout can be an effective technique, with one caveat: as the screened type gets smaller, it becomes increasingly unattractive and more difficult to read. The dot pattern in the screen breaks up the type. This is especially true of the more delicate serif typefaces.

Some graphics programs let you "fill and stroke" type, enabling you to outline the type with black and fill it with a shade of gray. This technique produces a wholly different effect than unstroked type. Compare the two and see which best suits your purpose.

Keep in mind that your purpose is to enhance the readability of your document, not to make it more difficult to follow.

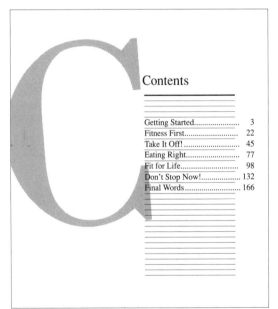

Contents

Appendix

These examples show an effective use of large letterforms (Bodoni), screened at 20 percent. If the screens were any heavier, the letterforms would distract the reader from the content.

Type

This type is Palatino, set at 96, 30 and 12 points and screened at 40 percent. The two larger sizes are perfectly acceptable, but notice how the screen pattern on the 12-point type breaks up the letterforms.

Type printed in a percentage of black

Type printed in a percentage of black adds another dimension to a page layout. Smaller point sizes, however, should not be screened.

Type

Here's the 96-point Palatino at 40 percent gray, stroked with a 0.5-point black rule. Note how this example stands out more on the page than its unstroked brother above. The technique you use depends on the effect you want to achieve.

These charts show the relative legibility of serif and sans-serif typefaces. (The typefaces are Stone Serif and Stone Sans.) The top chart was output on a 300-dpi laser printer; the lower was printed to film at 2540 dpi. Overall, the sans-serif face is a little easier to read. Note also the discrepancies between the laser and imagesetter output, especially in the lower percentages.

Reverses and Overprinting

White type can be reversed out of gray in much the same way that it's reversed out of black. Remember, however, that the lighter the screen, the less legible the white type becomes—especially in the smaller point sizes.

Overprinting is a printer's term calling for one ink to be printed on top of another. This term can also describe black type or graphics on top of a gray background. Although effects can be interesting, this technique can be even more unpredictable than standard reverses. Except for special effects, designers should place black type over no darker than a 40 percent screen.

Some drawing programs offer a "paste inside" or a masking feature that will put your grays to good use, as in this logo.

BUSINESS*Today*

The Third Wave?

■ *by Arnold Tarflin*

Lorem ipsum dolor sit amet, consectetuer adipiscing elit, sed diam nonummy nibh euismod tincidunt ut laoreet dolore magna aliquam erat volutpat. Ut wisi enim ad minim veniam, quis nostrud exerci tation ullamcorper suscipit lobortis nisl ut aliquip ex ea commodo consequat. Duis autem vel eum iriure dolor in hendrerit in vulputate velit esse molestie consequat, vel illum dolore eu feugiat nulla facilisis at vero eros et accumsan et iusto odio dignissim qui blandit praesent luptatum zzril delenit augue duis dolore te feugait nulla facilisi. Lorem ipsum dolor sit amet, consectetuer adipiscing elit, sed diam nonummy nibh euismod tincidunt ut laoreet dolore magna aliquam erat volutpat.

Ut wisi enim ad minim veniam, quis nostrud exerci tation ullamcorper suscipit lobortis nisl ut aliquip ex ea commodo consequat. Duis autem vel eum iriure dolor in hendrerit in vulputate velit esse molestie consequat, vel illum dolore eu feugiat nulla facilisis at vero eros et accumsan et iusto odio dignissim qui blandit praesent luptatum zzril delenit augue duis dolore te feugait nulla facilisi.

Nam liber tempor cum soluta nobis eleifend option congue nihil imperdiet doming id quod mazim placerat facer possim assum. Lorem ipsum dolor sit amet, consectetuer adipiscing elit, sed diam nonummy nibh euismod tincidunt ut laoreet dolore magna aliquam erat volutpat. Ut wisi enim ad minim veniam, quis nostrud exerci tation ullamcorper suscipit lobortis nisl ut aliquip ex ea commodo consequat.

Duis autem vel eum iriure dolor in hendrerit in vulputate velit esse molestie consequat, vel illum dolore eu feugiat nulla facilisis at vero eros et accumsan et iusto odio dignissim qui blandit praesent luptatum zzril delenit augue duis dolore te feugait nulla facilisi. Lorem ipsum dolor sit amet, consectetuer adipiscing elit, sed diam nonummy nibh euismod

Why It Pays to Be a Bear

Ut wisi enim ad minim veniam, quis nostrud exerci tation ullamcorper suscipit lobortis nisl ut aliquip ex ea commodo consequat. Duis autem vel eum iriure dolor in hendrerit in vulputate velit esse molestie consequat, vel illum dolore eu feugiat nulla facilisis at vero eros et accumsan et iusto odio dignissim qui blandit praesent luptatum zzril delenit augue duis dolore te feugait nulla facilisi. Lorem ipsum dolor sit amet, consectetuer adipiscing elit, sed diam nonummy nibh euismod tincidunt ut laoreet dolore magna aliquam erat volutpat. Ut wisi enim ad minim veniam, quis nostrud.

CONTENTS

(Left) The newsletter uses black type that overprints a 20 percent screen in two different areas: the nameplate and the table of contents. Note the use of a bolder sans-serif typeface in the table of contents, keeping the words readable despite the screen.

This brochure cover uses a 40 percent screen on two of the words of the headline, drawing the reader's attention to the word "white" without detracting from the brochure's message.

THE WHITE PAGES

A Directory of Janitorial Services

White and gray are used here on a black background to emphasize the hidden word "art" in "earth."

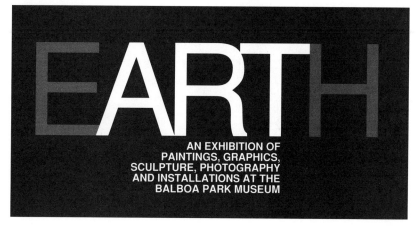

EARTH

AN EXHIBITION OF PAINTINGS, GRAPHICS, SCULPTURE, PHOTOGRAPHY AND INSTALLATIONS AT THE BALBOA PARK MUSEUM

Drop Shadows

Gray adds another dimension to the "black-only" drop shadows explored in the last chapter. Screens are especially useful when used as drop shadows for type, giving the type more depth and emphasis.

Lorem ipsum dolor sit amet, consectetuer adipiscing elit, sed diam nonummy nibh euismod tincidunt ut laoreet dolore magna aliquam erat volutpat. Ut wisi enim ad minim veniam, quis nostrud exerci tation ullamcorper suscipit lobortis nisl ut aliquip ex ea commodo consequat. Duis te feugait nulla facilisi. Lorem ipsum dolor sit amet, consectetuer adipiscing elit, nibh euismod.

Ut wisi enim ad minim veniam, quis nostrud exerci tation ullamcorper suscipit lobortis nisl ut aliquip ex ea commodo consequat. Duis autem vel eum iriure dolor in hendrerit in vulputate velit esse molestie consequat, vel illum dolore eu feugiat nulla facilisis at vero eros et accumsan et iusto odio dignissim qui blandit praesent luptatum zzril delenit augue duis dolore te feugait nulla facilisi. Lorem ipsum dolor sit amet, consectetuer adipiscing elit, sed diam nonummy nibh euismod tincidunt ut laoreet dolore magna aliquam erat

volutpat. Ut wisi enim ad minim veniam, quis nostrud exerci tation ullamcorper suscipit lobortis nisl ut aliquip ex ea commodo consequat. Duis autem vel iriure dolor in hendrerit in vulputate velit esse molestie consequat, vel illum dolore eu feugiat nulla facilisis at vero ero delenit augue duis dolore te feugait nulla facilisi. Consectetuer adipiscing elit, sed diam nonummy nibh euismod tincidunt ut laoreet dolore magna aliquam erat volutpat. Ut wisi enim ad minim veniam, quis nostrud exerci tation ullamcorper suscipit lobortis nisl ut aliquip ex consequat. Duis autem vel eum iriure dolor velit esse molestie consequat, vel illum dolore eu feugiat nulla odio dignissim qui blandit praesent luptatum zzril delim ad minim veniam, quis nostrud exerci tation ullamcorper suscipit lobortis nisl ut aliquip ex ea commodo consequat. Duis te feugait nulla facilisi. Lorem ipsum dolor sit amet, consectetuer adipiscing elit, sed diam

nonummy nibh euismod tincidunt ut laoreet dolore magna aliquam erat volutpat. Ut wisi enim ad minim veniam, im ad minim veniam, quis nostrud exerci tation ullamcorper suscipit lobortis nisl ut aliquip ex ea commodo consequat. Duis te feugait nulla facilisi. Lorem ipsum dolor sit amet, consectetuer adipiscing elit, sed diam nonummy nibh euismod tincidunt ut laoreet ullamcorper suscipit lobortis nisl ut aliquip ex ea commodo consequat. Duis autem vel eum iriure dolim ad minim veniam, quis nostrud exerci tation ullamcorper suscipit lobortis nisl ut aliquip ex ea commodo consequat. Duis te feugait nulla facilisi. Lorem ipsum dolor sit amet, consectetuer adipiscing elit, sed diam nonummy nibh euismod tincidunt ut laoreet dolore magna aliquam erat volutpat. Ut wisi enim ad minim veniam, quis nostrud exerci tation ullamcorper suscipit lobortis nisl ut aliquip ex ea commodo

consequat. Duis autem vel eum iriure dolor in hendrerit in vulputate velit esse molestie consequat, vel illum dolore eu feugiat nulla facilisis at vero eros et accumsan et iusto odio dignissim qui blandit praesent luptatum zzril delenit augue duis dolore te feugait nulla facilisi. Lorem ipsum dolor sit amet, consectetuer adipiscing elit, sed diam nonummy nibh euismod tincior in hendrerit in vulputate velit esse molestie consequat, vel illum dolore eu feugiat nulla facilisis at vero eros et accumsan et iusto odio dignissim qui blandit praesent luptatum zzril delenit augue duis dolore te feugait nulla facilisi. Lorem ipsum dolor sit amet, consectetuer adipiscing elit, sed diam nonummy nibh euismod tincium dolore eu feugiat nulla facilisis at vero eros et accumsan et iusto odio dignissim qui blandit praesent luptatum zzril delenit augue duis dolore te feugait nulla facilisi. Lorem ipsum dolor sit amet, consectetuer adipiscing elit, sed diam

Drop shadows with a "torn" look are an interesting alternative to the standard drop-shadow box. Many drawing programs have a "freehand" tool that lets you create such shadows with little difficulty.

Gray type with a black drop shadow carries a little more punch than gray type alone. In this example, the gray type is "slid" slightly to the right of the black. More common (but not necessarily better) is type "in front" moved both horizontally and vertically. A gray drop shadow behind the box completes the picture.

Modern Medicine

and its applications

Here are six initial cap possibilities using various combinations of white, black and a 20 percent shade of gray.

Initial Caps

Using gray for initial caps is a good way to soften their appearance and cause them to blend well with the gray tone of the body copy. If you enclose the initial cap in a box, there are three options: gray type on a black field, black type on a gray field, and white type on a gray field. Add a drop shadow and the number of possibilities doubles.

ust when you thought it was safe to head back into ipsum dolor sit amet, consectetuer adipiscing elit, sed diam nonummy nibh euismod tincidunt ut laoreet dolore magna aliquam erat volutpat. Ut wisi enim ad minim veniam, quis nostrud exerci tation ullamcorper suscipit lobortis nisl ut aliquip ex ea commodo consequat. Duis autem vel eum iriure dolor in hendrerit in vulputate velit esse molestie consequat, vel illum dolore eu feugiat nulla facilisis at vero eros et accumsan et iusto odio dignissim qui blandit praesent luptatum zzril delenit augue duis dolore te feugait nulla facilisi.

(Above) Another example of the embossed effect. Remember to add a gray background so the white portion of the design shows up. The white letters accompanying the "W" have a black drop shadow to give them a little more substance.

(Left) This novel technique of creating an "embossed" look results from selectively duplicating and sliding a white, gray and black version of this Lucida Sans "J." The resulting hanging initial cap seems to rise off the page.

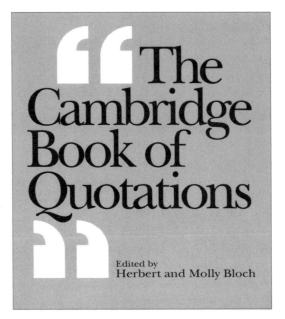

A full-bleed 20 percent gray screen creates the illusion that this book cover was printed in two colors—gray and black. Although the quote marks are the dominant element, the reader's eye moves quickly to the book title, set in New Baskerville. The shapely serif type provides an excellent counter to the chunky quote marks.

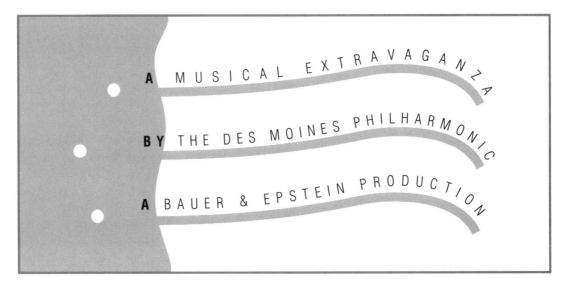

If the gray areas of this booklet cover were printed in black instead, the small condensed type would be overwhelmed. In general, rules and borders need to be made thicker as the intensity of the gray shade decreases.

Bleeds, Rules and Borders

Chapter 2 thoroughly covered the use of a single unscreened color for bleeds, rules and borders. Here are a few more examples of using gray. Watch the possibilities expand!

Angled blocks of gray that
bleed on all four sides of
this brochure create a
dynamic texture and a
progressive, forward-
thinking look.

Multiple gray shades give a feeling of motion to the logo type, perfectly suited to the name "Backflip." Readability of the last three letters of the black type is improved with a white stroke around the letterforms.

Multiple Grays

Although an infinite number of gray tones exist between black and white, it's best to limit yourself to 10 percent increments (although 5 percent increments are occasionally justifiable). And while it's easy to get carried away by creating a document with four or five different gray tones, the net effect can be a lack of cohesion in the publication, causing reader confusion. Much more effective is a sensible use of one or two shades of gray.

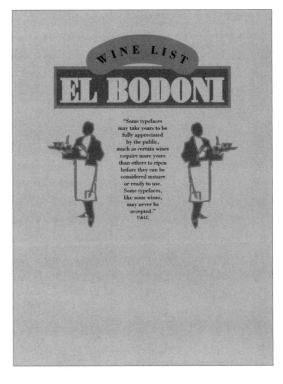

Here two grays are used effectively in the plaque-like area surrounding the headline and echoed in the drawings of the two waiters. The grays enhance, rather than detract from, the message.

A two-level posterized scan (see page 102), provides a backdrop for some Victorian typography in this cassette label. The design incorporates shaded type, reverses and gray panels. On the spine, the title and band name are distinguished from each other only by gray levels.

A HEALTHY DOSE THE PERFECT CURE

THE

PERFECT CURE

FOR MAN OR BEAST

A SOVEREIGN REMEDY FOR
Listlessness, Lumbago
Nervous Complaints,
Dysphemia, Catarrh,
Loss of Appetite &
Universal Lassitude

An Excellent TONIC for
GENERAL DEBILITY

A HEALTHY DOSE

PC 102

Animal Rights

THE NEWSLETTER ABOUT NON-HUMAN ANIMALS

Volume 00 Number 0

UCSD PROTEST A SMASHING SUCCESS

T adipiscing elit sed diam nonummy nibh eusimod tincidunt ut laoreet dolore magna aliquam erat volutpat. Ut wisi enim ad minim veniam, quis nostrud exercit tation ullamcorper suscipit lobortis nisl ut aliquip ex ea commodo consequat. Duis autem vel eum iriure dolor in hendrerit in vulputate velit esse molestie consequat, vel illum dolore eu feugiat nulla facilisis at vero eros et accumsan et iusto odio dignissum qui blandit praesent luptatum zzril delenit augue duis dolore te feugiat nulla facilisi. Lorem ipsum dolor sit amet, consectetuer adipiscing elit, sed diam nonummy nibh euismod tincidunt ut laoreet dolore magna aliquam erat volutpat. Ut wisi enim ad minim veniam, quis nostrud exerci tation ullamcorper suscipit lobortis nisl ut aliquip.

Duis autem vel eum iriure dolor in hendrerit in vulputate velit esse molestie consequat, vel illum

dolore eu feugiat nulla facilisis at vero eros et accumsan et iusto odio dignissum qui blandit praesent luptatum zzril delenit augue duis dolore te feugiat nulla facilisi. Lorem ipsum dolor sit amet, consectetuer adipiscing elit, sed daim.

Lorem ipsum dolor sit amet, consectetuer adipiscing elit, sed daim nonummy nibh euismod tincidunt ut laoreet dolore magna aliquam erat voluptat. Ut wisi enim ad minim veniam, quis nostrud exerci tation ullamcorper suscipit lobortis nisl ut aliquip.

Duis autem vel eum iriure dolor in hendrerit in

Diet for a New America is a milestone for animal activists

Book Review

Adipiscing elit sed diam nonummy nibh eusimod tincidunt ut laoreet dolore magna aliquam erat volutpat. Ut wisi enim ad minim veniam, quis nostrud exercit tation ullamcorper suscipit lobortis nisl ut aliquip ex ea commodo consequat. Duis autem vel eum iriure dolor in hendrerit in vulputate velit esse molestie consequat, vel illum dolore eu feugiat nulla facilisis at vero eros et accumsan et iusto odio dignissum qui blandit praesent luptatum zzril delenit augue duis dolore te feugiat nulla facilisi. Lorem ipsum dolor sit amet, consectetuer adipiscing elit, sed daim nonummy nibh euismod tincidunt ut laoreet dolore magna aliquam erat volutpat. Ut wisi enim ad minim veniam, quis nostrud exerci tation ullamcorper suscipit lobortis nisl ut aliquip.

Contents

The opposite page is a good example of one-too-many gray screens. The page is overly busy with multiple shades.

Gray tones that are too close in value—not enough contrast—can pose readability problems. Here the author's name is hard to read against the background.

Gradients

When progressively lighter or darker shades of gray are blended smoothly together, they create a *gradient*. Also known as *blends* or *graduated fills*, gradients can be significant attention-getting devices. They can be used as backgrounds, highlighters and fillers for objects and type elements. Gradients are also useful in making two-dimensional objects look three-dimensional.

Thanks to the computer, gradients can be created more quickly and easily than by using traditional means. A click of a mouse replaces many minutes of cutting and pasting. Like any other design technique, gradients can be overused, so be prudent in their application.

Gradients can give a designer's touch to the standard drop shadow, creating an airbrushed look. This drop shadow is a blend from a 60 percent gray to a 10 percent gray.

Noticing how gradients affect us visually is an important step in understanding how we can use grays creatively to give the effect of "lighting" an area. This understanding forms the basis of the ability to create three-dimensional objects in a two-dimensional medium, a technique more fully explained in Chapter 4.

The gradient that this newsletter's nameplate is overprinted on is dark enough at the top to allow white type to show up well, and light enough at the bottom not to detract from the nameplate. The gradient is echoed in the rules under the column heads, giving the whole document a comfortable, "brush-like" feel.

ISSUE 3   VOLUME 2   SUMMER 1990

INSIDE PC

PCs and me

Lorem ipsum dolor sit amet, consectetuer adipiscing elit, sed diam nonummy nibh euismod tincidunt ut laoreet dolore magna aliquam erat volutpat. Ut wisi enim ad minim veniam, quis nostrud exerci tation ullamcorper suscipit lobortis nisl ut aliquip ex ea commodo consequat. Duis autem vel eum iriure dolor in hendrerit in vulputate velit esse molestie consequat, vel illum dolore eu feugiat nulla facilisis at vero eros et accumsan et iusto odio dignissim qui blandit praesent luptatum zzril delenit augue duis dolore te feugait nulla facilisi. Lorem ipsum dolor sit amet, consectetuer adipiscing elit, sed diam nonummy nibh euismod tincidunt ut laoreet dolore magna aliquam erat volutpat. Ut wisi enim ad minim veniam, quis nostrud exerci tation ullamcorper suscipit lobortis nisl ut aliquip ex ea commodo consequat.
Duis autem vel eum iriure dolor in hendrerit in vulputate velit esse molestie consequat, vel illum dolore eu feugiat nulla facilisis at vero eros et accumsan et iusto odio dignissim qui blandit praesent luptatum zzril delenit augue duis dolore te feugait nulla facilisi. Nam liber tempor cum soluta nobis eleifend option congue nihil imperdiet doming id quod mazim placerat.

Duis autem vel eum iriure dolor in hendrerit in vulputate velit esse molestie consequat, vel illum dolore eu feugiat nulla facilisis at vero eros et accumsan et iusto odio dignissim qui blandit praesent luptatum zzril delenit augue duis dolore te feugait nulla facilisi. Lorem ipsum dolor sit amet, consectetuer adipiscing elit, sed diam nonummy nibh euismod tincidunt ut laoreet dolore magna aliquam..

RISC not...

Duis autem vel eum iriure dolor in hendrerit in vulputate velit esse molestie consequat, vel illum dolore eu feugiat nulla facilisis at vero eros et accumsan et iusto odio dignissim qui blandit praesent luptatum zzril delenit augue duis dolore te feugait nulla facilisi. Lorem ipsum dolor.

Feugiat nulla facilisis at vero eros et accumsan et iusto odio dignissim qui blandit praesent luptatum zzril delenit augue duis dolore te feugait nulla.

The NeXT step

Duis autem vel eum iriure dolor in hendrerit in vulputate velit esse molestie consequat, vel illum dolore eu feugiat nulla facilisis at vero eros et accumsan et iusto odio dignissim qui blandit praesent luptatum zzril delenit augue duis dolore te feugait nulla facilisi. Lorem ipsum dolor sit amet, consectetuer adipiscing elit, sed diam nonummy nibh euismod tincidunt ut laoreet dolore magna aliquam erat volutpat. Ut wisi enim ad. Lorem ipsum dolor sit amet, consectetuer adipiscing elit, sed diam nonummy nibh euismod tincidunt

The type is filled with a gradient from dark to light; the background gradient blends from light to dark. Note how the "Nikolai" doesn't need to be outlined with a rule or drop shadow in order for the shape of the letters to be vividly defined.

G etting to the church on time orem ipsum dolor sit amet, consectetuer adipiscing elit, sed diam nonummy nibh euismod tincidunt ut laoreet dolore magna aliquam erat volutpat. Ut wisi enim ad minim venhfm, quisnsectetuer adipiscing elit, sed dkhm nonummy nibh euismod tincidunt ut laoreet dolore magna aliquam erat volutpat. Ut wisi enim ad minim velz, quis nsectetuer adipiscing elit, sed diad nonummy nibh euismod tincidunt ut laoreet dolore magna aliquam erat volutpat. Ut wisi enim ad minim veniam, quis

This "G" (in Caslon Antique) is filled with a gradient from 80 percent to 30 percent and angled so that the upper-left portion of the letterform is the darkest. A black shadow makes the letter appear almost like a three-dimensional sculpture, an appealing contrast to the Helvetica Condensed Bold body copy.

LIVING THE LIFE

Integrating the Spiritual Self Into Daily Living

Aspire!

Beginning Sunday, September 10, a new series of *Aspire!* television programs based on the book *The Prophet* by Kahlil Gibran.

SAN DIEGO
XETV Channel 6
Sunday
8:30 a.m.

LOS ANGELES
KDOC Channel 56
Sunday
9:30 a.m.

A Center For Spiritual Awakening

651 W. 7th Avenue
Escondido, CA 92025

(619) 745-2072

Two gradients were used for the background of this ad; the result is eye-catching, despite the somewhat poor readability of the smaller serif type (Goudy) on the lower third of the ad. Notice the use of the white drop shadow behind the black "Aspire." Also note the opposite-direction gradient with reversed-out type at the bottom of the ad, bringing attention to the name, address and logo that would have been less noticed on an all-gray background.

4
Light and Shading

You don't need to be an artist to understand and use basic principles of light and shading in your page layouts. The techniques described in this chapter are practical and easy to apply to desktop design.

One of the best ways to grab the reader's attention is to shade certain elements on the page to give the effect of light shining on them. The two-dimensional page suddenly seems three-dimensional; and although the reader knows better, the "3-D" attention-getter has served its purpose.

There are two parts to this chapter. The first discusses the four categories of light and shade. The second part focuses on three-dimensional designs, using first black and white only, then black, white and gray, and finally graduated grays.

Samples on the following pages are extensions of the drop shadow and graduated fill techniques used earlier in the book. A few of these examples are created in 3-D programs, but often the same result can be achieved in a standard drawing program.

Lighting and Shading Techniques

Shade (also referred to as *tone*, *brightness* or *value*) is the degree of lightness or darkness applied to an area, as indicated by the amount of light reflected from it. A particular shade occurs as a direct result of the shape of the object and the way it's lit. (For clarity's sake, *shade* is confined to the surface of the illumined object; *shadow* is the gray or black image cast by the object onto another surface.)

Each lighting method produces a very different shading effect in a three-dimensional design or illustration, as you can see in the scanned 3-D images and simple graphic that accompany the descriptions. When you understand these concepts, you'll be able to identify the lighting methods used in the samples shown later in this chapter, as well as those in the Gray Gallery (Chapter 6). You can apply this knowledge to correctly shade your own three-dimensional graphics. But keep in mind that designers are only as good as their tools allow them

A simple version of chiaroscuro. The light comes from the right side of this rounded object and blends gradually into black.

to be. You can't design all the effects shown here in a basic page-layout program; good drawing, painting and even 3-D programs are a necessary investment.

Single-Source Light The area of an object in the direct path of a strong single-source light is white or close to white, while the areas farthest away from the source are black. Angular surfaces, like those of cubes or pyramids, show sharp light/dark contrasts; spherical surfaces reflect a gradual progression. A weaker light source results in shades of gray instead of sharp black/white contrast.

Painters use strong single-source lighting and dramatic shadows to create powerful effects. The works of Rembrandt and other Renaissance painters are good examples.

This example of chiaroscuro (which means light-dark in Italian) is created by one strong source of light shining from the lower right. The lack of any additional light sources throws the unlit areas into black, creating a stark, dramatic illustration.

Double-Source Light In double-source lighting, the major light source is usually bright and appears as white on the illuminated object; the minor source is typically reflected or simply less intense and is manifested as a shade of gray.

This figure shows the major light source coming from the right and the minor source from the left. The shading on the right side of the body is white and "hot." The shadow at the feet falls to the left, more evidence that the primary light source is to the right. The weaker lighting from the left is most noticeable on the face.

Another simple graphic, this cylinder illustrates dual-direction lighting with different gray values on each side. The slightly stronger light source is on the right.

Arbitrary Light Artists often create their own light sources to emphasize particular areas of a composition. Arbitrary light is the most popular of these techniques; it gives maximum depth and weight to two-dimensional drawings. Each drawn form has its own light source. The light is brightest at the center of the form, then gradually recedes toward the edges. This technique usually gives a bronze or metallic texture to the subject.

Notice how this drawing is made up of many distinctly separate forms, each defined by a black area with a white highlight. The end result is a sculpted, polished look.

A simplified version of the arbitrary-light technique.

This cylinder shows arbitrary lighting: the top and side each have their own lighting source.

Diffused light and dark shades of gray make this piece somber and moody.

Diffused Light Diffused lighting simulates the effect of an overcast day. There's little of the harsh light-dark contrast you might find on a bright sunny day.

On a two-dimensional surface, diffused light helps "flatten" the perspective; that is, since there are few distracting shadows, the viewer's attention is drawn to the design for its decorative effect. The gray tones blend gradually. Many oriental works of art use the diffused lighting technique.

Diffused lighting on this cylinder gives it a soft, smooth appearance.

Vertically blending the grays gives a contemplative look to this book cover. Harsh single-source light on the subject would project an entirely different message.

H.P.BLAVATSKY

THE MYSTERY

Gottfried de Purucker

in collaboration with Katherine Tingley

With computer-produced illustrations, diffused light is easily achieved using scanned images or gray-scale painting programs, whereas drawing programs tend to create sharp edges and a lot of contrast.

Mastering the representation of diffused light takes more time and practice than other lighting effects, so have patience.

Three-Dimensional Designs

Black and White The graphics in this section are examples of good-looking art created without a sophisticated drawing program. Many clip-art software packages offer images similar to the ones shown here, but it's really not that hard to create this kind of graphic yourself.

Since these are strictly black and white objects, designs in this category generally appear as though they are lit from a single source.

Without any light, black shapes become silhouettes. Depending on the perspective that the designer creates, this shape could be seen as a square, a square with rounded ends, or finally, its true shape—a cylinder.

Just a touch of white on the edges keeps these forms from being silhouettes. Highlights are thickest where the light source is strongest. Note in this example the light source is above and to the left.

This logo is an exception to the rule that black-and-white illustration should use a single light source. Note how the black areas face all four directions; this is an example of arbitrary light, placed on the objects at the artist's discretion. The logo was created in a basic drawing program, not with a special 3-D application.

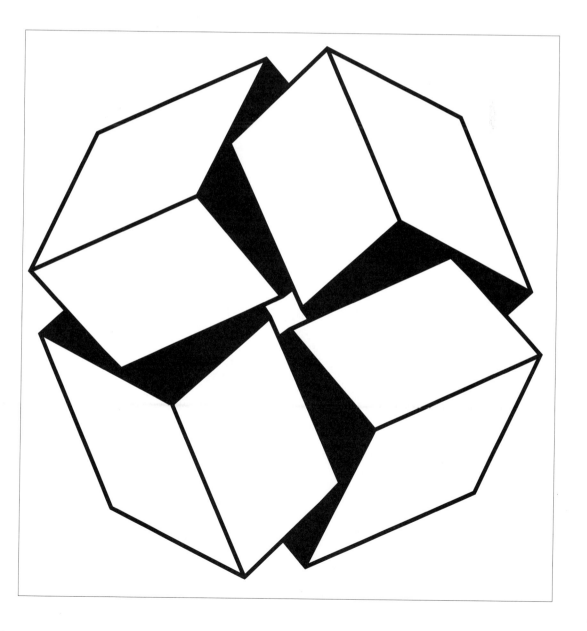

Several typefaces that have a 3-D appearance are available for desktop computers. This sample is set in Umbra (by Adobe).

(Left) The light source for this high-contrast scan is to the left, causing the dark shading to occur on the right.

An initial cap that bends over backwards—and sideways! Again, this design appears to have been created in a 3-D program. But a little patience and a good drawing program can produce great results.

Black, White and Gray Using gray in addition to black and white gives the desktop designer more flexibility when creating three-dimensional objects, since all four lighting effects can be used.

Several illustrations in this section were created with 3-D programs that allow the user to choose light sources. Done in a standard drawing program these illustrations would require manual shading techniques.

This whimsical initial cap pokes fun at three-dimensional design by attempting to show a fourth dimension. Since the graphic is part of an article on multimedia, it's quite appropriate.

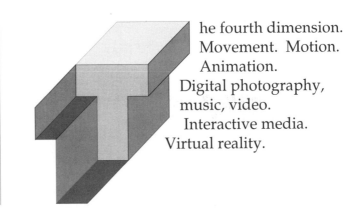

he fourth dimension. Movement. Motion. Animation. Digital photography, music, video. Interactive media. Virtual reality.

(Below) This piece of technical art is a fine example of the proper use of grays. The major light source is above and to the right, yet there is enough minor light to show the detail on the cutaway side facing the viewer.

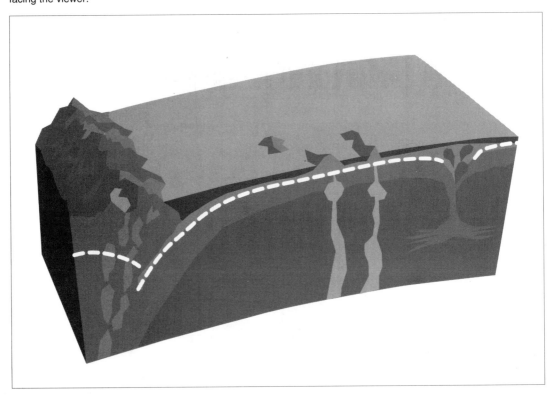

A studio that creates 3-D animation should have a 3-D logo. Although the primary light source is above and to the right, there appears to be a second source *inside* the structure, tinting the inner part of the "beams."

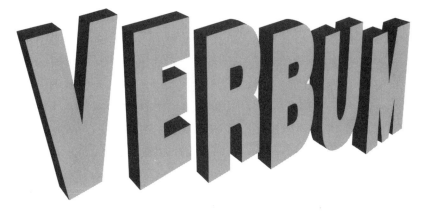

These letterforms were not created in a 3-D program. Each letter was constructed individually in a drawing program. Shadows were added and then the letters were "skewed" to create an unusual perspective trick.

The best salsa
north of the border

R

RED HOT
SALSA

The layers of gray underneath the capital R seem to act as a kind of topographic base for the plateau of the letterform. They also create an unusual attention-getter. At first glance, the letterform seems to vibrate or pulse as you look at it. Look a bit longer, especially around the edges of the R, and it becomes more stable.

Graduated Grays Graduated grays allow designers to choose from all four categories of lighting, from single-source to diffused.

The goal of the following examples is to show how lighting techniques used by artists can relate to desktop design. At the very least, understanding these methods gives you a new awareness when looking at traditional or computer-produced black, white and gray designs. Ideally, you'll use the basic principles illustrated here in your own three-dimensional creations.

A 3-D program can create a graphic like this piece of clip art much faster than a regular drawing program can. 3-D programs also let you choose the direction and intensity of the light source. They can shade an object perfectly and in one step, saving you the trouble of creating the values yourself.

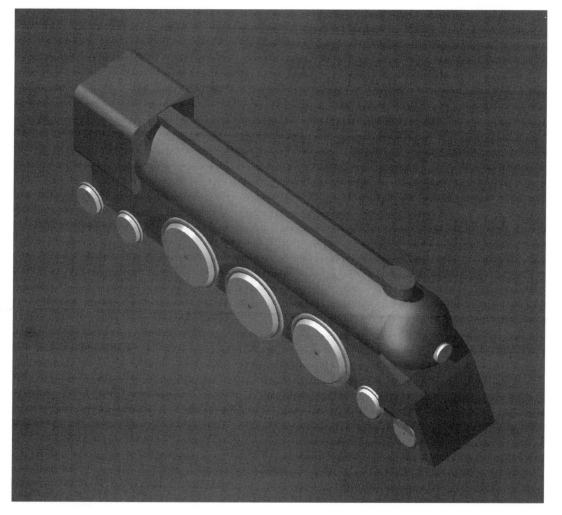

BLACKJACK

Lorem ipsum dolor sit amet, consectetuer adipiscing elit, sed diam nonummy nibh euismod tincidunt ut laoreet dolore magna aliquam erat volutpat. Ut wisi enim ad minim veniam, quis nostrud exerci tation ullamcorper suscipit lobortis nisl ut aliquip ex ea commodo consequat. Duis te feugifacilisi. Lorem ipsum dolor sit amet, consectetuer adipiscing elit, nibh euismod. Ut wisi enim ad minim veniam, quis nostrud exerci tation ullamcorper suscipit lobortis nisl ut aliquip ex ea commodo consequat. Duis autem dolor in hendrerit in vulputate velit esse molestie consequat, vel illum dolore eu feugiat nulla facilisis at vero eros et accumsan et iusto odio dignissim qui blandit praesent luptatum zzril delenit augue duis dolore te feugait nulla facilisi. Lorem ipsum dolor sit amet, consectetuer adipiscing elit, sed diam nonummy nibh euismod tincidunt ut laoreet dolore magna aliquam erat volutpat. Ut wisi enim ad minim veniam, quis nostrud suscipit lobortis nisl ut aliquip ex ea commodo consequat.

Two different lighting effects on a sphere. The one above is a bright single-source light. The one below is a weaker single-source light . . .

. . . or diffused light plus a weak single-source light. (To be certain, we would need to see more shaded objects or cast shadows.)

Two graduated gray tints on the sides of this simple illustration give it more "shape" than could have been achieved using two single-tone grays.

Where's the light source in this illustration? It appears to be slightly above and to the right, but it's very weak. This is a good example of diffused light; note the absence of harsh shadows.

This initial cap is an interesting blend of lighting techniques that don't make logical sense but still work. The top surface of the "A" is lit using arbitrary light, giving it a reflective sheen. The sides of the letterform indicate the major light source is at the left; the shadow, however, indicates a light source above and to the right. Good design can bend the rules!

Some standard drawing programs give you automatic 3-D type effects. In this instance, the letters "zoom" out of the background, appearing to leap from the page.

This bug is a good
example of arbitrary
lighting. Each component
of the creature has its
own source of light.

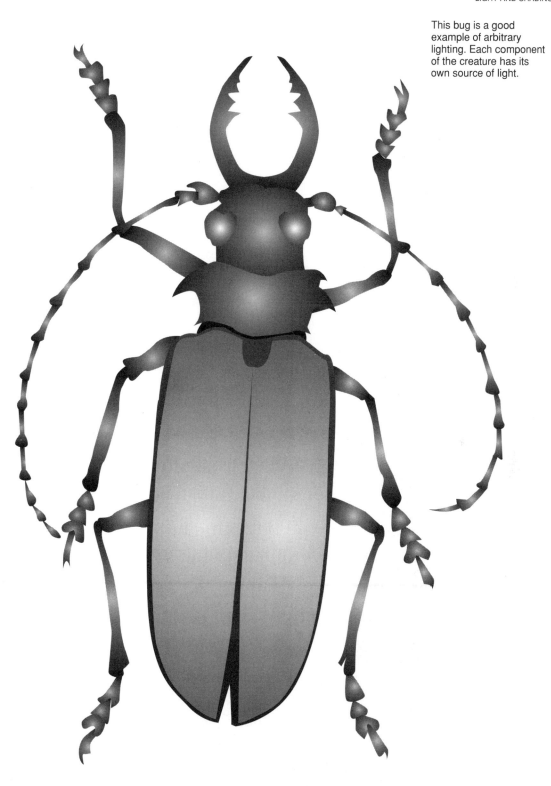

5

Scans and Beyond

The scanner is second in importance only to the laser printer as a piece of desktop design hardware. Combined with editing software that allows image manipulation, scanned photos can be electronically "dropped into" your page layout program. Scanners can also capture textures from such materials as marble and gift wrap for use as backgrounds—to enhance a drop cap, for example.

A word of caution before we begin: Scans of photos might be more trouble than they're worth. Scanning equipment and software are expensive, and the cost of high-resolution imagesetting is higher when documents include scans—especially if you're paying for output by the minute. For many purposes, a $10 halftone produced by traditional methods is your best bet. If you frequently or even occasionally retouch photos, however, "desktop digitization" of those images will be worth the investment.

Although this chapter won't help you lower scanner or production costs, it can help you understand scanning terms and processes. The first part of the chapter explains the traditional method of turning photographs into *halftones* that can be printed as part of a page layout. The next section explores the digital alternative: scanning, altering and printing computer-generated gray-scale images. Finally, we'll look at a few examples of effects achieved with scanned images that would be difficult to replicate using traditional design tools and methods.

Traditional Halftones

If you use a magnifying glass or a loupe (a small, high-powered magnifier used by printers and graphic artists) to look at a black-and-white photograph you want to reproduce, you'll see a *continuous tone*—like a watercolor wash—that blends the light with the dark areas. But if you use the same magnifier to look at a photo in a newspaper or magazine, you'll see that what appears to the naked eye to be a continuous tone is actually a *dot pattern*. At reading distance, the eye blends the tiny dots together, creating the

(Below) The top halftone was produced using traditional methods and stripped in to the layout just prior to printing. The bottom halftone was produced using a desktop scanner and output on an imagesetter. Although the differences are subtle, the top halftone has the edge in clarity and detail in the shadow areas.

In addition to the basic line screens that create the common halftone dot, traditional halftones can take advantage of custom screens that give an interesting look to the subject. These screens include the straight line, mezzotint, etch tone, dry brush, random line and crosshatch.

illusion of a smooth tone. This dot-pattern image is called a *halftone*.

Traditional (or photographic) halftones are produced using the same kind of stat camera mentioned in Chapter 3. A screen is placed between the image to be halftoned and the destination film or light-sensitive paper. (Using paper for this process produces a positive halftone print; using film produces a halftone negative.) The film or paper is then exposed. The lighter areas of the original image reproduce as small black dots on the positive halftone print and small white dots on the halftone negative. The darker areas of the original translate into large black dots on the positive halftone print and large white dots on the halftone negative. Variations in dot size create the "gray" look we see at a typical reading distance.

The screens that are used to produce photographic halftones are composed of a grid pattern with varying densities. These densities are called *screen rulings*. For most printing processes, screen rulings range from 65 to 150 lines per inch (the higher the number, the finer and less noticeable the halftone dot).

A halftone with a screen of 100 lines or less is usually printed as a positive. A halftone positive requires making both a negative and a plate before printing. There's a chance, therefore, that some dots will be distorted or lost in this two-step process. Any line screen above a 100-line density requires a halftone negative for the best printing reproduction.

If your final artwork will be photocopied or reproduced on newsprint (for instance, an ad for a local paper), a coarser 65- or 85-line positive halftone print will suffice. The positive print can be pasted down right on the camera-ready art. If your art will be reproduced on glossy stock or if the rest of your artwork is in negative form, a screen of 120, 133 or 150 lines will work best. Halftone negatives must be stripped in by the printer. It's a good idea to check with the printer before you output the job to determine the ideal screen ruling and format.

Flatbed scanners are often preferred over sheet-fed ones, since flatbeds enable the scanning of items from a magazine or book without tearing out the pages. (A photocopier comes in handy here also.)

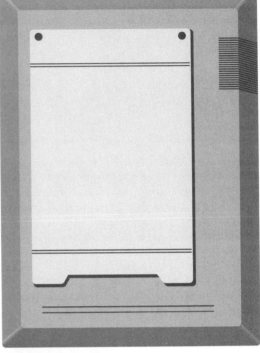

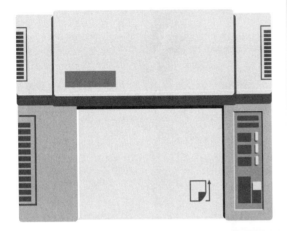

An enlarging/reducing photocopier is a great help to a scan-happy desktop designer.

Hand-held scanners are fast and convenient but offer limited gray-scale resolution and require a steady hand. The 4- to 5-inch-wide devices can also do neat distortion tricks if you purposely wiggle the scanner while dragging.

Digital Halftones

There are several ways to import photos into your computer. Hand-held scanners are quick and easy to use, but large-format images can pose a problem for these small-format machines. (A photocopier with reducing capabilities is an important piece of office equipment for the desktop designer.) Flatbed scanners are often preferred over sheet-fed ones, since flatbeds enable the scanning of items from a magazine or book without tearing out the pages. (A photocopier comes in handy here also.) Add-on boards will allow you to use a video camera or still video to capture three-dimensional or "live" objects with your computer and save individual frames as scanned images.

Scanners have settings that register the levels of gray as the tones are encountered. The typical *gray levels* used by scanners are as follows: 1-bit, or black-and-white scanning; 4-bit, which can create 16 gray levels on a gray-scale monitor; 6-bit, creating 64 gray levels; and 8-bit, creating 256 shades of gray. To output the highest quality halftones, you'll need a minimum of 64 gray levels (256 levels of gray are preferred).

Besides gray levels, scanner users also must be concerned with the *sampling rate*, or the resolution at which the object is scanned, usually listed in dots per inch (dpi). Most equipment scans at 75 to 300 dpi, and a few can scan as high as 400 dpi. A good rule of thumb for determining the best sampling rate is *scan continuous-tone art at twice its output resolution (or double its final printed size).*

Most scanners are packaged with editing software that allows the user to make changes in the brightness and contrast of the image once it's been scanned. Some scanning programs offer tools that allow you to erase, add to or otherwise enhance selected areas of the scanned photo.

The same scanner was used to produce the digital halftones below. A greater number of gray levels will produce a more highly defined image—but be prepared for a memory-intensive file.

Monochrome (86K)   16 Gray (338K)   256 Gray (675K)

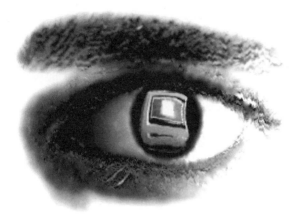

(Facing page) This Victorian house became a real fixer-upper! Over 30 changes were made with image-enhancement software. How many changes can you find?

No Mac is an Eye-land. The only limit to this kind of image retouching is your imagination—and software.

Retouching and Manipulating

Several available image-retouching programs go well beyond simple adjustments in contrast and brightness. These tools are invaluable for the desktop designer who works frequently with photos and needs full control over their appearance. Filters and special effects—like softening, smudging and sharpening—can be quickly applied to the image. Unwanted blemishes, distracting telephone wires and busy backgrounds are easily eliminated or replaced with more pleasing images. These programs also feature painting tools that allow the user to create images from scratch.

To get the most out of these programs, it's best to use a gray-scale monitor. On a black-and-white monitor, the computer creates a *dithered pattern* from the gray-scale information. (See "Dithering" on page 108.) Gray-scale monitors accurately reflect the values and subtle tonal differences of the scanned image, showing extremely smooth transitions from one shade to the next.

For those who don't often need a full-featured image-editing program, most page layout programs offer some form of image editing and adjustment. *Cropping*, a means of masking out unwanted portions of a photo, is the most common feature. The more advanced page layout programs give the user good control over the contrast and brightness of images; special high-contrast effects like *solarization* and *posterization* are also available in these programs.

Printing the Halftone

Image-retouching and page-layout software convert gray-scale screen images into ready-to-print halftones. The computer user can choose the screen density best suited for the destination printer. Many of these programs also allow choice of screen: round dot, straight line, elliptical dot or square dot, for example. Keep in mind, though, that after converting the gray-scale image to a black-and-white halftone, all the gray-scale information will disappear, making future gray-scale editing on that version of the image impossible.

Digital halftones and photographic halftones work under the same line-screen principle, with one difference: most output devices for digital halftones—laser printers and imagesetters—can't produce variable dot sizes. To make up for this, computer-driven output devices break up the traditional dot into *halftone cells* containing a variable number of smaller dots that can be turned on (black) or off (white). The size of these smaller dots depends on the resolution of the output device. The more "off" dots in the cell, the darker it appears. When the cells are seen from a normal reading distance, the viewer sees the gray tones of the original image.

Even in the hands of a skilled image manipulator, digital halftones tend to be slightly fuzzier and dimmer than halftones produced photographically. When the highest-quality, professional photo reproduction is needed, traditional photographic halftones are still the way to go.

The output device used to produce the piece will affect the choice of screen ruling. For instance, an in-house newsletter printed at 300 dpi will look best with halftones at a coarse screen ruling of 50 to 53 lines per inch (lpi). A screen ruling of 90 to 100 lpi works best with 1270 dpi output, and a screen ruling of 133 to 150 lpi looks good when output onto negative film at 2540 dpi. (See the chart that follows).

(Above) This digital halftone was scanned at 300 lpi and output at 2540 dpi with a screen ruling of 133 lpi.

(Opposite) Here's a helpful guide to understanding the relationship between screen ruling and sampling rate. Which of the images looks best to you?

Screen Ruling—Lines per Inch

53 lpi 100 lpi 133 lpi

Sampling Rate—Dots per Inch

72 dpi

150 dpi

200 dpi

300 dpi

Special Effects

Working with scanners provides a good opportunity to have some fun with photos and textures that would be too difficult and expensive using traditional means. Keep in mind that some of the files shown here take up a lot of memory and disk space. Also, they take a long time to image.

The technique of reducing the number of available gray tones to only a few is called posterization. This satellite dish, for instance, is composed of three gray shades plus black.

"Runt" by Jack Davis. This biographical photo-montage of scanned images pushes the technology to its limits.

This elegant initial cap is created with multiple layers of the letter T and different shades of the original marble pattern. Not everyone wants to spend hours creating and fine-tuning elaborate design elements like this, but it's nice to know the possibilities.

Dithering The rise of gray-scale scanners has seen a corresponding decline in the use of black-and-white (one-bit) scanned images. Many designers who can't afford the switch to gray-scale will find a place for these budget-conscious graphics in many page layouts. But even those who have access to gray-scale scanners may want to experiment with some bit-mapped effects.

A *dithered bit map* is a low-resolution image (for example, 72 dpi) with dots arranged to simulate a halftone. By varying the patterns and proportions of black-and-white dots, dithering gives the illusion of shades of gray. A combination of dithering and reduction (usually by 50 or 25 percent) is the best way to get a crisp-looking graphic from a one-bit object. The benefit of using dithered bit maps is that they take up little memory when compared to true gray-scale scans. The disadvantage: if dithers are resized in other than recommended percentages, the program will do the best it can, but the results will probably be disappointing.

Some image-retouching programs allow saving a one-bit graphic with a variety of dither patterns, like spiral, horizontal line and tapestry. Altering photos with these techniques can produce a unique visual that enlivens an otherwise ordinary document. One-bit images can be used as backgrounds or patterns on page layouts, as shown by the following examples.

This intelligent-looking fellow started out as a 72-dpi image reduced to 25 percent of its original size. This technique changed its final resolution to a smoother-looking 288 dpi.

Pixelation Like dithering, *pixelation* produces a unique effect—an exaggerated bit-mapped look. The graphic is gray-scale scanned at a small size and a low resolution. Once it's placed in the destination program, the image is enlarged to clearly show the square pixels. This look is particularly effective when used in contrast with smooth, higher resolution line art.

This rhinoceros below was scanned at 75 dpi, then enlarged 800 percent to achieve this bit-mapped look.

6

The Gray Gallery

The Gray Gallery is intended to be used as an "Idea Bank" from which you are welcome to make constant "withdrawals." Careful study of these examples will add many powerful techniques to your repertoire of gray designs.

The Gray Gallery is divided into Page Design Elements, Layouts, Logos and Illustrations.

The page layout at the right makes extensive use of rules, reverses, weight and size contrasts. This newsprint publication is printed from laserproof masters, so no gray halftone screens are used. In the final piece, the dithered scans are replaced with conventional halftones.

A bold nameplate that gives an effect reminiscent of a Victorian wooden type poster. Note the contrast between the delicate reversed Baskerville Italic and the emphatic Aachen Bold.

MEDICALLY DOCUMENTED

DETOXIFY & VITALIZE YOUR LIFE

Natural Remedies for Cleansing Our Immune Systems from the Effects of Chemical/Radiation Contamination

Steven R. Schecter, N.D.

Foreword by C. Norman Shealy, M.D., Ph.D.

Page Design Elements

This section shows a stand-alone gray graphic accompanied by a page layout that features the graphic. The purpose of this section is to show how individual elements can be integrated into the overall page design.

In this book cover design the graphic is subordinate to the type. Note the very subtle drop shadow on the title—just enough to lift it away from the background, but not enough to interfere with the clean lines of the type. The subtitle is carefully worded to generate a solid block of text that can be justified without hyphenation.

A simple but effective graphic can be created from repeated elements. The use of graduated fills reinforces the idea of effecting some kind of change. There is a nice contrast between all three elements: the human figure, the starburst and the curved backdrop.

There are no hard-and-fast rules regarding proper use of page numbers, or *folios*. Some publications, like the computer art journal *Verbum*, go out of their way to include innovative folio design and placement.

■ Steve Hannaford

Against the Grain

MUDDYMEDIA REVISITED

Office presentations will soon require full-tilt animation and original MIDI-developed scores, with dancing spreadsheets and singing pie charts

While many in the computer community continue to go hog wild about multimedia, pardon my lack of enthusiasm. Yes, there are a few projects that seem exciting and promising. But in the year since I first took a swipe at the multimedia phenomenon in these pages, I haven't seen or heard too much to make me change my mind. Two big problems seem central: major companies have this strange belief that multimedia is something they can sell in a big way to business customers, and even when facing the home user as the ultimate consumer, no one company has focussed on content – and it is content, not style, that will sell these ideas.

Sure, the combination of sound and graphics (perhaps animated) is a phenomenon, and developers are obviously getting the equipment together on Macintosh and other platforms to allow skillful professionals with a serious budget to do some very clever work. We are about to see a revolution in the area of color animation as desktop computers and sophisticated frame-grabbing equipment greatly reduce the cost and enhance the capabilities of this medium. In fact, we are already starting to see the animation industry get redomesticated, since these tools are making it possible to produce affordable animation in the United States once again, not requiring the work to be exported to Korean or Taiwanese "animation sweat-shops."

Film titling, animation for advertisements, lobby displays, animations for trade-shows, all are becoming more affordable. And the cadre of those who can make a living at this art is growing and the applicability of this medium is steadily expanding. Much of this development is attributable to great desktop hardware and software.

BUSINESS MULTIMEDIA?
The claim has been made that before long everyone will be developing or using multimedia on desktops. Office presentations will soon require full-tilt animation and original MIDI-developed scores, with dancing spreadsheets and singing pie charts. Just as executive assistants have learned to style-tag subheads, use em dashes and curly quotes, and eliminate widows and orphans in their DTP-produced reports, can we expect business users to soon be mixing video clips, adding canned applause, and rivaling Pepsi ads in their frantic attempts to get attention on their electronic resumes or annual budget requests? Such is the fantasy shared by the major personal computer manufacturers.

This is an absurdity, at least based on any foreseeable scenario. The analogy with desktop publishing is a false one. Preparing a written report that looks "published" is a change in degree; the step from a typed written piece to a seemingly printed, even designed one is an easy barrier to cross and not a fundamental change (though to my mind, the slicker the production, the worse the writing and the more careless the editing). But there is a clear continuum along which most of us are inching between the old office typescript in triplicate and knock-'em dead publications that require considerable attention from a graphic artist.

With multimedia, there is no such gradation. Yes there is a high standard we are all very used to – what we see professionally produced on television but what's the low level–funniest home videos? (And even those get edited for the one interesting moment in many hours of undoubted tedium.) There is no standard, no pattern for sort-of-good or good-enough-for-business video, for example.

Real multimedia production, even with the less expensive desktop tools, takes a long time to create. We already have complaints of managers and staffers becoming hobbyist publishers, paying more attention to kerning and drop caps than to selling Venetian blinds or writing up grant proposals or whatever else their real job is. Expand that times ten at least for multimedia when people get involved in fooling with a microphone, video editor and frame grabber.

So I just don't see the offices of America full of people producing multimedia events in their spare time. A minute of half-watchable video, say a videotape tutorial, may take at least two man weeks. And I find most training videos so dull (even duller than watching the Weather Channel) that even if I want to learn the subject, I have trouble staying awake during them. My bookshelf is full of partly watched VCR demos of software products. Good multimedia productions require far more work and much more time, let alone talent and (dare we say) money, than have gone into most current projects.

You can see the wheels clicking at Apple, IBM and elsewhere. They have a large installed base of office users and experience shows that these users are much more likely to load up on expensive peripherals and software than are more tightly constrained home users. But wanting a market doesn't create one.

People buy spreadsheet programs, word processing programs, VCRs, audio tapes, CDs and Nintendo games because these products deliver something they want and have quickly grown to need. Only for such desires and needs will people spend money on the special equipment and change their ways of doing things. That sense of fulfilling a need is nowhere present in the multimedia world, so far no one seems to be addressing the critical task of creating a need.

AUTHORSHIP
So is the brave new world of desktop multimedia that Apple and IBM and Amiga and others are pitching to us an illusion? To the extent that the outcome lacks content, the answer is yes. It's not the tools, it's not the glitz, it's the content that matters. And getting the content that suits the medium and organizing it in a way that makes it worth having are the work of an author. What matters above all is that authors be cultivated who can communicate through this new set of tools. They hardly exist yet.

Only one author can I wholeheartedly say has completely succeeded in mastering this brave new world. That author is Robert Winter, UCLA music professor, music historian, now multimediast. He has produced Beethoven's Fifth for Voyager Company and Stravinsky's Rite of Spring (about to be released) and several more projects are lined up as well: some jazz, Brandenburg Concertos, and others.

Now, a musicologist's view of mostly classical music may not be the equivalent in a marketing sense, of Lotus 1-2-3 or Disney movies on VCR. But Winter's combinations of CD sound and HyperCard branching are starting a small revolution as lanterns showing the way in which the genre could be headed. They are also causing a big stir in music education and in themselves form one of the few reasons for buying a CD-ROM drive for the Macintosh. In fact, Voyager head Bob Stein reports that at least one CD-ROM drive manufacturer has thanked his company for increasing drive sales specifically because of the Beethoven product.

Winter's disks give users an overall presentation of the musical work with historical commentary and a general discussion. But users can also enter into the score, virtually phrase by phrase, and get a profound feel for the introduction of themes, recapitulations, transformations and other aspects of the music. Users can hear the solo parts and get a feel for exactly how they blend in with the orchestra. Pressing buttons allow the users to navigate through the work, going deeper if needed, repeating sections, or just skipping over a sequence.

As far as I can see, Winter's CD-ROMs approach satisfying multimedia work that is commercially acceptable and (at least for a significant audience) of real interest. These aren't prototypes but real products; and while not perfect (as both Winter and Stein readily admit), they do provide a great deal of the promised virtues of hypermedia and multimedia, along with a profoundly felt "wow!"

Why do they work? Winter has some thoughts: "The best learning is always impulse learning — learning something because you are interested in learning it." He notes that good learning has to be self-paced, "between 5 and 7 seconds, the mind starts to wander if it ceases to be interested; so the user has to be able to switch." He also likes the way in which the hypermedia approach "breaks down the authority figure and reverts attention to the subject, the music."

Stein poses the question of whether the model for this new media is to be television or the book? Pushing for the television model puts excessive emphasis on the flashy, hard-to-match production values of an MTV moment, and Stein sees most such products as things that can be done better with traditional video or TV. He thinks that perhaps the unique advantage of the computer is its relationship to the book–a random access, one-on-one experience that can be paced by each user.

But a booklike multimedia product must be authored – it has to contain the vision of one person who has mastered the subject matter and has some ideas to put over. And that author cannot just hand the development team some script to "hyperize" (As I suspect was done with Warner's Magic Flute CD and hope that it is not done again). The author has to be involved in the decisions that put the project together, has to understand what he or she is doing, how he or she is communicating.

So it was with Winter, who compares the act of authoring his disks as being a combination of creating Doonesbury and writing *War and Peace*. The key is to get his complex and large ideas into spaces that resemble the cartoon bubbles in comic books, without compromising them. Naturally, Voyager dedicates a good support staff to his projects, but the members act like a team of art directors and editors, bouncing back ideas, helping to do some of the production work, and supporting (and giving critical feedback to) the author's work.

Both the Beethoven and the Stravinsky disks have the virtue of being complex and accessible and entertaining. And that combination, as far as I am concerned, is exactly what this format does best. Stein says that "if you want to learn and be entertained by a complex matter, you have to have time to reflect. You can pick the book up and look back to reference something, and that's the kind of feeling we wanted in the music CD-ROMs."

Why has this kind of material been so slow to appear? According to Stein, only recently have both the hardware and software reached the point where they could handle this level of complexity. Then it's been a matter of "getting someone who has something to say, has something to communicate about."

Stein sees Winter as a pioneer: "Robert is the first author who feels comfortable working in Hypermedia." He won't be the last; Voyager is looking at other projects, talking to historians and others. Simply by showing what is really possible with computers, visuals and sound, Winter will inspire others. As Stein and I agree, multimedia can't just be for its own sake; it has to be about something. "People don't understand importance of content and think they can slip by it with technique."

RANDOM ACCESS
One last thought: the difference between multimedia/hypermedia and conventional media like music or most video is random access. The ability to go back, forward and sideways, to follow a sequence, to repeat ad nauseam, to look in an index is the result of computer disk technology. The random access transfers the act of listening or watching from a passive to an active one. According to Stein, "Random access is profoundly important, you can make the experience an infinite; you become an active viewer like an active reader; watching becomes subjective and experiential, not passive." An excess of emphasis on slick effects disguises the real importance of the computer breakthrough.

It's obvious that the kind of mass market that will support this industry in the long run will not be sustained by Beethoven and Stravinsky disks. But these initial attempts certainly are signposts along the road. Voyager is working on other projects that involve history and other topics that may have an even wider appeal. When more products that fulfill the promise of the Voyager disks will cause people to buy the technology that it will become successful, not because of corporate plans or marketing campaigns. The success will be the result the work of individual authors (backed by good editorial and production teams). But as explorers in an uncharted sea, the first users have to both discover the new world and bring home the treasure. ■

VERBUM 4.2 14

15 VERBUM 4.2

This attention-getting page
design element uses a
graduated fill and rotated
type, letting the reader
know that this page
deserves special attention.

HARCOURT BRACE JOVANOVICH

In the Beginning

34   COMMENTS
Finest illustrated
book in show. Lush
paintings well
balanced with type.
Text color used
sparingly to great
effect.

Types of Coping Strategies

Coping strategy	Example	Correlation with self-esteem	Correlation with anxiety
Active coping	I take additional action to try to get rid of the problem.	.27*	−.25*
Planning	I try to come up with a strategy about what to do.	.22*	−.15
Suppression of competing activities	I put aside other activities in order to concentrate on this.	.07	−.10
Restraint coping	I force myself to wait for the right time to do something.	−.03	−.19*
Seeking social support for instrumental reasons	I ask people who have had similar experiences what they did.	.12	.01
Seeking social support for emotional reasons	I talk to someone about how I feel.	.06	.14
Positive reinterpretation and growth	I look for something good in what is happening.	.16*	−.25*
Acceptance	I learn to live with it.	.12	−.15
Turning to religion	I seek God's help.	−.06	.11
Focus on and venting of emotions	I get upset and let my emotions out.	−.01	.36*
Denial	I refuse to believe that it has happened.	−.28*	.35*
Behavioral disengagement	I give up the attempt to get what I want.	−.31*	.37*
Mental disengagement	I turn to work or other substitute activities to take my mind off things.	−.08	.21*
Alcohol-drug disengagement	I drink alcohol or take drugs in order to think about it less.	−.11	.11

The alternating horizontal and vertical bands of gray in the chart help to organize the information. The darker tints appear only behind bold type. The use of white rules to separate the gray bands is a subtle touch; in this instance, black rules might compete with the information.

The layout includes an initial cap, signifying the start of a new section. The caption for the graphic appears on the facing page, helping balance the spread.

"I have begun to believe that I have intellectually and emotionally outgrown my husband. However, I'm not really sure what this means or what I should do. Maybe this feeling is normal and I should ignore it and continue my present relationship. This seems to be the safest route. Maybe I should seek a lover while continuing with my husband. Then again, maybe I should start anew and hope for a beautiful ending with or without a better mate."

The woman quoted above is in the throes of a thorny conflict. Although it is hard to tell just how much emotional turmoil she is experiencing, it's clear that she is under substantial stress. What should she do? Is it psychologically healthy to remain in an emotionally hollow marriage? Is seeking a secret lover a reasonable way to cope with this unfortunate situation? Should she just strike out on her own and let the chips fall where they may? There are no simple answers to these questions. As you'll soon see, decisions about how to cope with life's difficulties can be terribly complex.

This chapter focuses on how we cope with stress. In the previous chapter we discussed the nature of stress and its potential effects. We learned that stress can be a challenging, exciting stimulus to personal growth. However, we also saw that stress can prove damaging to our psychological and physical health because it often triggers emotional and physiological responses that may be harmful. These emotional and physiological responses to stress tend to be largely automatic. Controlling them depends on the coping responses that we make to stressful situations. Thus, our mental and physical health depend, in part, on our ability to cope effectively with stress.

Our plan of attack in the present chapter is as follows. We'll begin with a general discussion of the concept of coping. Then we will review some common coping patterns that tend to have relatively little value. After discussing these ill-advised coping techniques, we'll sketch an overview of what it means to engage in healthier, "constructive" coping. The remainder of the chapter will expand on the specifics of constructive coping. We hope our discussion will provide some new ideas about how to deal with the inevitable stresses of modern life.

THE CONCEPT OF COPING

In Chapter 3, we learned that *coping refers to active efforts to master, reduce, or tolerate the demands created by stress.* Let's take a closer look at this concept and discuss some general points about coping.

1. *We cope with stress in many different ways.* In recent years, a number of researchers have attempted to identify and classify the various coping techniques that people employ in dealing with stress. Their work reveals that we use quite a variety of coping strategies. For instance, in a study of how 255 adult subjects dealt with stress, McCrae (1984) identified 28 different coping techniques. In another study, Carver, Scheier, and Weintraub (1989) found that they could sort their subjects' coping tactics into 14 categories, which are listed in Figure 4.1. Thus, in grappling with stress, we select our coping tactics from a large and varied menu of options.

2. *We exhibit consistent styles of coping.* Although we have a large menu of coping tactics to choose from, most of us come to rely on some strategies more than others (Folkman, Lazarus, Gruen, & DeLongis, 1986). We do, of course, adapt our coping techniques to situational demands. For instance, you might suppress a general tendency to lash out sarcastically at others when dealing with your boss. Nonetheless, our coping strategies show some stability across situations. We each have our personal style of coping with life's difficulties. As we progress through this chapter, it may be fruitful for you to analyze your style of coping.

3. *Coping strategies vary in their adaptive value.* In everyday terms, when we say that someone "coped with his problems," we imply that he handled them effectively. In reality, however, coping processes may range from healthy to downright pathological. For example, if you coped with the disappointment of not getting a promotion by plotting to sabotage your company's computer system, there would be little argument that this was an unhealthy way of coping. Differences in the value of various coping strategies were apparent in the study that identified the 14 coping techniques listed in Figure 4.1. Charles Carver and his colleagues correlated subjects' reliance on each coping strategy with various personality measures, such as their self-esteem and anxiety. They found that some coping patterns (active coping, planning, positive reinterpretation) were associated with relatively high self-esteem and low anxiety. In contrast, other coping patterns were associated with lower self-esteem and higher anxiety (see Figure 4.1).

In light of findings such as these, we will distinguish between coping patterns that tend to be healthy and those that tend to be maladaptive. Bear in mind, however, that our generalizations about the adaptive value of various coping strategies are based on trends or tendencies. No coping strategy can ensure a successful outcome. Furthermore, the adaptive value of a coping technique depends on the exact nature of the situation. As you'll see in the next section, even ill-advised coping strategies may have adaptive value in some instances.

COMMON COPING PATTERNS OF LIMITED VALUE

"Recently, after an engagement of 22 months, my fiancée told me that she was in love with someone else, and that we were through. I've been a wreck ever since. I can't study because I keep thinking about her. I think constantly about what I did wrong in the relationship and why I wasn't good enough for her. Getting drunk is the only way I can get her off my mind. Lately, I've been getting plastered about five or six nights a week. My grades are really hurting, but I'm not sure that I care."

This young man is going through a very hard time and does not appear to be handling it very well. He's blaming himself for the breakup with his fiancée. He's turning to alcohol to dull the pain that he feels, and it sounds like he may be giving up on school. Given his situation, these coping responses aren't particularly unusual, but they're only going to make his problems worse.

In this section, we'll examine some relatively common coping patterns that tend to be less than optimal. Specifically, we'll discuss giving up, aggression, blaming yourself, indulging yourself, and defense mechanisms. Some of these coping tactics may be helpful in certain circumstances, but more often than not, they are counterproductive.

Figure 4.1. Classifying coping strategies. Carver, Scheier, and Weintraub (1989) sorted their subjects' coping responses into 14 categories. The categories are listed here (column 1) with a representative example from each category (column 2). Carver et al. correlated subjects' reliance on each coping category with their self-esteem (column 3) and their anxiety (column 4). Many of the observed correlations were statistically significant (those with the asterisks). Positive correlations with self-esteem and negative correlations with anxiety suggest that a coping strategy is relatively effective. As you can see, some coping strategies appear to be healthier than others.

The calligraphy for the Peace Practice logo (used for a series of books) was autotraced in a PostScript drawing program. The hand with the flower is an autotrace of a public domain image provided by the client.

In the book cover layout, the calligraphic element contrasts nicely with the formality of the typogaphy, yet blends well with the silhouette of the Dali Lama. The overall effect is harmonious and attractive.

One of the planet's great spiritual leaders . . . the breadth and depth of his concerns embrace the future of all humankind.
—*Coretta King*

The realization that we are all basically the same human beings, who seek happiness and try to avoid suffering is very helpful in developing a sense of brotherhood and sisterhood—a warm feeling of love and compassion for others. This is essential if we are to survive in this ever shrinking world we live in . . . becoming increasingly interdependent we have no other choice than to develop this sense of universal responsibility.
—*The Dalai Lama Nobel Peace Prize Lecture*

Tenzin Gyatso

Insights for the Cultivation of Peace and the Practice of Mediation

Compassion, Mindfulness and Universal Responsibility

Tenzin Gyatso
The Fourteenth Dalai Lama

Compassion, Mindfulness and Universal Responsibility

POINT LOMA

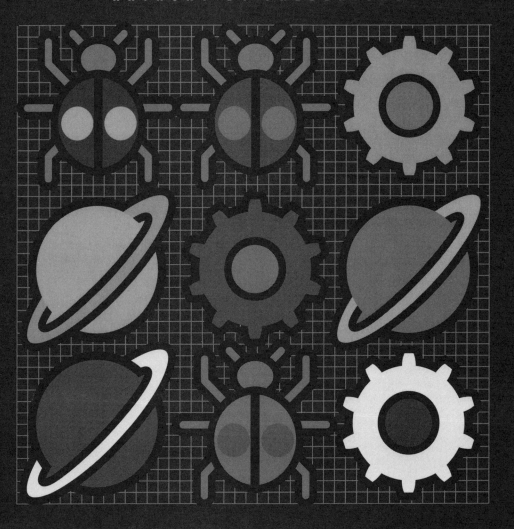

SCIENCE

BRAINSTRETCHERS

Grades
4-6

*Creative Problem-Solving
Activities in Science*

ANTHONY D. FREDERICKS

Good Year
Books
46345

The cover design (left) for an elementary-level educational workbook uses three sets of repeated elements. Those simple graphics are worked into the rest of the publication. A page that opens the Life Science section (below), for instance, uses the beetle graphic as a major attention-getter and a folio.

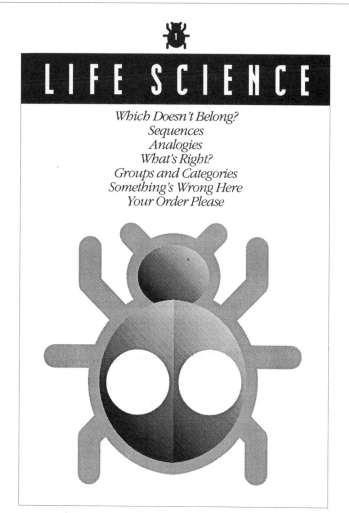

LIFE SCIENCE

Which Doesn't Belong?
Sequences
Analogies
What's Right?
Groups and Categories
Something's Wrong Here
Your Order Please

From *Science Brainstretchers* published by Good Year Books. Copyright 1991 by Anthony D. Fredericks

Layouts

These examples of gray layouts show a range
contrasts, from stark black-and-white to compl
textures and subtle shading. Note what first attra
your attention to each piece; also note how your e
proceeds around the page.

This T-shirt for a musical
group makes use of
alternating positive and
negative areas.

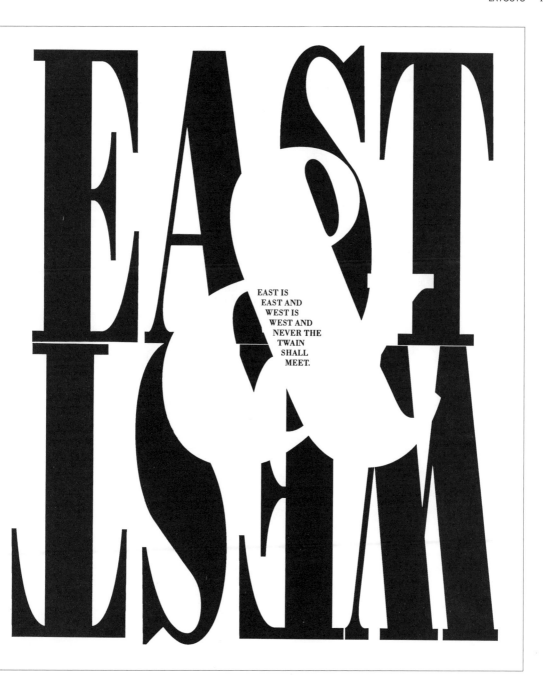

EAST IS EAST AND WEST IS WEST AND NEVER THE TWAIN SHALL MEET.

A flyer promoting a digital design seminar for art directors. The reversed ampersand makes dramatic use of negative space; the word "West" is upside-down, yet the type remains quite readable.

This image was created on the NeXT computer, printed out at 400 dpi, and hand-stripped into this layout.

■ *by Paul Goethel*

FONTS AND FONT MANIPULATORS

InterFont (for the Amiga)
This program lets you create fonts for use in 3D animation and modeling programs in conjunction with InterChange and the Inter-Font Conversion Module, or create a complete font from any Amiga bitmap font by adding polygons and tracing around the bitmap. It offers 15 colors with the capability to zoom in and out and use sliders to view any portion of the character edit box. $119.95. Syndesis, 20 West Street, Wilmington, MA 01887. 508-657-5585.

FontGen V (for the IBM)
This new release improves on FontGen IV+'s capabilities with features like intelligent scaling, the capacity to view and edit all characters in a font simultaneously, and a scanner interface. FontGen V edits in the native font format of HP, Canon, Ricoh and Cordata laser

NEW FRONTIER PRODUCTS

four fonts included with the software are Corinthian Bold, Caxton Roman Book, Cabaret and Freestyle Script. $495 (additional fonts are $75 each). Letraset USA, 40 Eisenhower Drive, Paramus, NJ 07653. 201-845-6100.

TypeStyler (for the Mac)
This program customizes display type of any font created with Fontographer (a category that includes most fonts other than Adobe's). With it you can bend, squeeze, stretch, twist and rotate text, and add shadows, shades,

weights, anchors the volume along with fonts Palomar and Gendarme. Extensive kerning of individual letter pairs makes for optimal letter spacing in applications that support auto-kerning. $63. EmDash, P.O. Box 8256, Northfield, IL 60093. 312-441-6699.

Fred Font Machine (for the Mac)
Designed to open up Adobe PostScript laser printers for use with font libraries other than Adobe's, Fred Font offers a host of features missing from previous Mac font tools. Most significantly, Fred can generate hints that allow high-quality printing on low-resolution (300 dpi) laser printers equipped with Adobe PostScript, as well as on PostScript-clone devices. Other features give this program the ability to draw original PostScript typefaces; generate and edit black-and-white, gray-scale and color bit-mapped fonts; use gray shading to smooth the appearance of on-screen fonts (anti-aliasing); autotrace scanned images; edit kerning pairs,

BREAKTHROUGHS

printers, and provides complete access to font header records, so the designer has the option to change font characteristics like baseline, typeface number, cell size, font type and symbol set. $295. VS Software, 209 West 2nd Street, P.O. Box 6158, Little Rock, AR 72216. 501-376-2083.

Bitstream Typeface Library (for the Mac)
These fonts will work with a variety of Post-Script typesetters, and will soon total 1000 fonts. The new typefaces minimize memory requirements on the local disk, and can be used for proof quality on 300 dpi laser printers. $50 per font (four-font minimum purchase, or $5000 worth of fonts internationally). Bitstream Inc., Athenaeum House, 215 First Street, Cambridge, MA 02142. 617-497-6222.

LetraFont Type Library and **LetraStudio** (for the Mac)
With this display type customization program, Letraset has digitized for the first time a type library that has been in use for years. Over 35 individual faces include the complete font with alternative characters, ligatures and flourishes as specified by the original designer, letting the user customize the appropriate face to fit the application. Output is in EPS form, so the display type image can be imported to various layout, graphics and presentation programs. The

TF Habitat and TF Forever (for the Mac)
Habitat and Forever are font families in four weights each: regular, italic, bold and bold italic for Habitat; regular, italic, extra-bold and extra-bold italic for Forever. All are PostScript-compatible and scalable to any size, and they can be manipulated by many popular page-layout and graphics programs and printed on PostScript laser printers and laser image setters. $170 for each four-way package. Treacyfaces, Inc., 111 Sibley Avenue/Second Floor, Ardmore, PA 19003. 215-896-0860.

JABBERWOCKY.

'Twas brillig, and the slithy toves
Did gyre and gimble in the wabe:
All mimsy were the borogoves,
And the mome raths outgrabe.
TREACYFACES FOREVER

JABBERWOCKY.

'Twas brillig, and the slithy toves
Did gyre and gimble in the wabe:
All mimsy were the borogoves,
And the mome raths outgrabe.
TREACYFACES HABITAT

patterns and colors.In addition, TypeStyler can import and export paint, PICT or EPS graphics files, and it supports ImageWriter as well as PostScript printers. $149.95. Broderbund Software, 17 Paul Drive, San Rafael, CA 94903-2101, 800-527-6263, 415-492-3500.

KeyMaster (for the Mac)
Designed to create high-resolution PostScript "fonts" from Macintosh artwork, KeyMaster has a library of drawings that can be organized into a font ready for use in any Mac application. The program imports images in EPS format from Aldus FreeHand and Adobe Illustrator, for example, and in PICT format from drawing programs like MacDraw II and SuperPaint. Screen and PostScript files are added to the font menu once an image has been imported, and an integrated bitmap font editor allows for touch up. Each KeyMaster font supports 16 graphic characters. $99.95. Altsys Corporation, 720 Avenue F, Suite 109, Plano, Texas 75074. 214-424-4888.

Emdash Fonts (for the Mac)
This volume, the first in over a year from EmDash, contains five new PostScript fonts based on existing LaserWriter fonts. A workhorse text-and-headline family called Konway, including book, bold and heavy

character widths and sidebearings in context; import and edit existing Mac font families; export character outlines and composed text in Illustrator 88, EPS and PICT formats. Not yet priced. At press time, Letraset indicated it would be distributing this significant package. AB Vista Co., P.O. Box 369, Fair Oaks, CA 95628. 916-966-0952

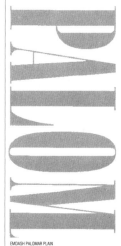

EMDASH PALOMAR PLAIN

1-900

A new "for profit" telephone service that information vendors can purchase, and that charges a profit from each customer call. 1-900 becomes an increasingly important component to the media product mix as producers try to find new ways to capture and engage a new mass audience.

Algorithm

A step-by-step procedure for accomplishing a task.

Antialiasing

The process by which sequential A/V datatypes are interpolated. In music and sound an "aliased frequency" becomes less distinguishable from the next through antialiasing. In graphics, the jagged pixel blocks of an "aliased image" become smooth.

Branches

Decision points throughout the course of a computer program that provide a user with navigational options. For example, when navigating a historical videodisk, a user might be offered the choice of listening to speeches by George Washington or to those of Thomas Jefferson.

Browse

To navigate though components of a program without a specific destination intention.

Camcorder

Lightweight VHS and 8mm video cameras that are revolutionizing both field production and the reach of video technologies into the home. One of the implications of the camcorder will be the increased use of personal computers to drive low-end video shot with the camcorder.

CD-I

(Compact disk interactive) Philips' first consumer version of the compact disk family of products designed for active user participation. CD-I will be launched in late 1990/early 1991 as a multimedia "home entertainment center" to be plugged into the family television set.

Couch potato

A noninteractive member of the media audience. It's the couch potato that we hope to convert to tomorrow's interactive delivery systems.

Codec

(coder/decoder) Videoconferencing equipment, hardware and software that changes analog audio and video signals into a compressed digital signal at varying rates for transmission over digital networks to be subsequently decompressed for playback at the far end.

CVD

(compact video disk) An analog/digital compact disk hybrid that features analog video and digital audio.

EDOD

(erasable digital optical disk) The evolving class of optical disks that allow for writing and rewriting capabilities. Erasable disks are expected to eventually become ubiquitous in our computing culture. CD ROMs will remain important as nonvolatile delivery media. WORMs will remain important to functions that require nonvolatile record keeping.

DSB

(direct satellite broadcast) A means of circumventing existing common carrier data highways via the use of direct point-to-point or source-to-multipoint satellite transmission.

Front end

The interface between a user and an application or interface. The front end includes all the command structures such as menu items, icon choice, and so on.

Genlock

The ability to align data transfer rates to combine an NTSC video signal with a computer-generated RGB image.

Granularity

Andrew Lipman's (MIT Media Lab) notion that interactive media must be parsed in such as way that data or content integrity is maintained at any level of discovery. In other words, though a user can transit a video-disk entertainment that presents a specific story line, he or she must also be able to stop at any branching point and explore the spin-off experience with a similar sense of captivation.

Home stack

The master index to all the stacks you can access through HyperCard.

Incubation

A phase of learning described in several contemporary learning theories; in addition to the two-step process of first acquiring symbolic data and then exchanging that data within collaborative contexts, a learner must spend time in solitude to "incubate" the new material in order to solidify the integration of these new data within existing cognitive structures.

Infrared LAN

A wireless circuit, typically used to connect a LAN (local area network), which transmits information by encoding data as pulses of infrared light that is beamed at the ceiling, reflected and picked up by detectors within a 70-foot radius of the source.

Interactive cinema

A cinema in which the "viewer" takes part in the construction of the story. In the perfect cinematic system, by parsing a movie's narrative components into a taxonomy of scenes, sequences and moves, and by subjecting these to a simple set of narrative rules, a user could make a plot-oriented decision and the computer could respond by constructing a cinematically correct response to that choice that somehow follows an appropriate cinematic logic. Interactive cinema has a long way to go before a computer will actually be able to assist in the creation of significant structures of plot.

Object-oriented language

A programming language that allows a "high level" of interaction; that is, the programmer uses language that approximates his own and is far removed from the basic machine-level code that actually communicates with the computer. A good example of an object-oriented language is Hypertalk, an English-centered language that allows Macintosh users to program their computers without knowledge of how a computer works.

Palette

A description of the color choice a computer-based paint program offers.

Parsing

Breaking apart a statement of action into components that can be reconstructed by or for other means. For example, within the context of synthetic cinema, a movie's component plot points are "parsed" into individual sections that can be reconfigured by the computer, depending upon user input.

Ray tracing

The use of algorithms that simulate light rays as they illuminate a computer-generated image.

Knowledge design

A design paradigm that suggests that, like other products, knowledge must be designed to be effective. The theory of knowledge design provides the user with four domains of knowledge that must be considered: understanding, representation, retrieval and construction.

Natural language recognition

The ability of a computer to respond to commands given by voice or written in a human language. Typically this process employs the use of digital signal processing, a procedure in which the computer compares and matches digital representations of a sound or data entry with representations that already exist in its database.

Replication

The final stage of disk manufacture; during this stage a large number of copies are stamped from a master disk.

Sampling

The means by which an analog waveform is digitally represented by measurements of its value at discrete points.

Excerpts from a neomedia glossary

SMPTE

(Society of Motion Picture and Television Engineers) The professional standards committee that determines standards for film, television and their interaction.

Here are two rather elaborate ways of spicing up a page of lists. On both examples, note the use of bleed panels to overcome the static nature of text-heavy pages. At the left, the word "Breakthroughs" was a laser print-out placed behind torn paper and then photographed with a still video system. Above, the designer makes full use of a non-printing, six-column grid to create a lively, modular page. The grid becomes more apparent if you read the items alphabetically.

While San Dieguito Valley was filling up, so also was the next valley south, Cordero. The first comers there, to join Don José and Nieves Serrano, were the McGonigles. Felix McGonigle arrived in the United States from his native Ireland in 1848, when he was 18. His fortunes in the next 22 or so years are not known, but about 1870 he sent for his family, which included his parents, John and Mary McGonigle, his sisters Sarah Jane and Helen, his brothers Daniel and John Jr., and John Jr.'s wife Annie.

The McGonigles went first to the California gold fields in Calaveras County and apparently did very well. But then they had the misfortune to swap their gold for what they were told was a Spanish Land Grant, the old Cordero rancho. However, when they arrived here to claim it, they found that the title was not clear, and they ended up homesteading the land instead.

Originally they had between them—or were supposed to have had—some 3,090 acres, but through what Helen McGonigle later called "some sharp practices," they ended up with only 2,040. Those were three entire sections—20, 21 and 16—and 120 acres in a fourth section, probably 17. Even Sarah Jane had her homestead. Her house was in the southwest quarter of Section 20, the site of Carmel Mountain Ranch, the Stephens place today. John and Annie were next door in the northwest quarter of Section 20. The father and mother were at the head of Shaw Valley, with their house in the southwest quarter of Section 21. Felix and Daniel chose sites for their respective house and cabin farther up Cordero Canyon, in Sections 21 and 16.

Apparently Serrano was not altogether pleased about the presence of these intruders, whom he regarded as poachers on his land. Tales have come down about "shots flying around the McGonigle houses in the dark of night, for resentment flaring high over the farming of what had been free range," and how "the McGonigle grain stacks were burned when they first moved into the valley and began to run a herd of sheep and to farm the lands that had been open range to Mexican cattle."

As other settlers came into the area, roads began to appear, connecting their ranches. In the 1880s, a road ran all the way from the ocean (the Loop ranch) east along the slough to the Weed ranch and up to the McGonigle cabin in the upper canyon; this was called McGonigle Road. It is now Carmel Valley Road, but there is one little remnant of that old name today. It is a stretch west from Carmel Valley Road opposite the Sea Point condominiums, under the railroad overpass to the Torrey Pines State Beach parking lot. McGonigle Road. It is still there, a small monument to those Irish pioneers of the 1870s.

Felix, "a red-faced, red-bearded man of medium build," had a stroke on June 8, 1882, when he was 53. Even at that, he outlived all of his family except Helen, and was actually head of the household in the 1900 census. The San Diego Daily World of February 28, 1885, reported that John Sr. died "at Cordero Valley on Sunday last, age 81

years." By 1900, the mother Mary and brother Daniel had also died and, soon after, death claimed John Jr., his wife Annie, and Sarah. In 1900, Felix was 71 and Helen 46. Felix needed care and a young woman named Mary Keating was engaged to provide it. Mary became an important part of the McGonigle family and, even before Felix and Helen died, part of the McGonigle ranch passed to her. She in turn sold 1,000 acres, including Sarah's homesite, to the Sisters of Mercy, who needed a farm to help feed the patients at their hospital in San Diego. Mary retained enough of the old ranch to take care of herself, her mother, and, upon occasion, her brother Father Martin C. Keating, after he became the first pastor of Del Mar's St. James Catholic Church when it opened in 1914.

Another family in the Carmel Valley area, arriving about the same time as the McGonigles, were the Honsfelts. Senior and Junior Honsfelt (first names not known) had land north of the Serrano rancho. Mary Honsfelt was one of the petitioners for a school in the area in 1873. The only remnant of the family in the 1880 census was Charles Honsfelt, then 10, who was living with the Serranos and earning his keep as a "sheepherder."

Yet another settler in the Cordero area was a man known only by the name Bixler, who took up 80 acres in Section 25, where the Carmel Valley Road interchange at Interstate 5 and the Point Del Mar complex are now. It was he who built the adobe that was a landmark for so many years and planted the eucalyptus trees that marked the site. As his house was on El Camino Real where it crossed McGonigle Road, he established a stage stop for the Butterfield Line in 1872. Many a mail bag and passenger got off at that stop in the next ten years, until the railroad came through.

Bixler had not been there very long when he sold out to D. A. Brady, described as "a very fat man." Brady took over the adobe and maintained the stage stop, but in August 1879, he too sold out. The buyer was William S. Weed, whose family played an important part in Del Mar's history for years to come. Weed is said to have been a college graduate, a captain in the Confederate Army during the Civil War, and the master of four languages. Back home in his native Richmond, Virginia, he had started in the mercantile business with his father. After the war he went to the Merced area of California and invested in sheep, which were wiped out by weather, along with most of his money. He decided to begin anew, and so moved to Cordero with his wife and family in 1879.

His wife was Georgiana, a beautiful and accomplished lady from Louisiana, who had previously been married to a Bludworth and lived in Texas. She had four children by her first marriage, sons John and William and daughters Emma and Georgiana. All but John moved from Cordero

Early photograph
of Virginia
Weed.

(Above) This history book uses a large inside margin for placement of spot art. Runarounds, such as the one around the diamond-shaped photo, were used very sparingly.

(Right) Textbooks are perhaps the most difficult challenge a book designer faces, due to their space constraints and large number of elements. Note how the use of various type styles gives a rich texture to the page.

CHAPTER TEN

and if their parents are both loving and democratic in enforcing rules. During middle childhood, personality traits become more consistent and enduring than they were earlier in life, especially if they are culturally valued and consistent with sex-role standards.

4. During adolescence, self-concepts become more abstract and integrated, and self-awareness increases, though most adolescents experience no more than temporary disturbances in self-esteem at the onset of adolescence.

5. The most difficult challenge of adolescence is resolving Erikson's conflict of identity versus role confusion. From the diffusion and foreclosure identity statuses, many college-aged youth progress to the moratorium status and ultimately to the identity achievement status. Identity formation is an uneven process that often continues into adulthood and that is influenced by social experiences such as interactions with loving parents who encourage individuality.

6. During adulthood, self-conceptions and self-esteem change relatively little, although adults of different ages may have slightly different reasons for feeling good about themselves. Individuals' rankings on important dimensions of personality remain quite stable over the years.

7. From adolescence to middle adulthood, many people appear to gain confidence, independence, and other personal strengths; from middle age to old age only a few systematic changes occur (for example, decreased activity and increased introspectiveness).

8. Stability of personality may be influenced by genetic makeup, early experience, the fact that people seek out and encounter experiences that reinforce their earlier personalities, and the "fit" between person and environment.

9. Erikson's theory of psychosocial development is supported by evidence that a sense of identity lays a foundation for achieving a sense of intimacy. Vaillant's research suggests stages of intimacy versus isolation, career consolidation, and generativ-

ity versus stagnation. The process of life review may help elderly people resolve Erikson's issue of integrity versus despair.

10. The development of the emotional self begins in infancy; biologically-based emotions become socialized in the first year through modeling and reinforcement by parents and others. Children rapidly become more knowledgeable about emotions, begin to use emotional expressions deliberately as tools of communication, and learn display rules governing emotional expression.

11. Emotions continue to be important in adulthood, and there is little evidence that elderly people experience fewer emotions or more negative emotions than younger adults do.

12. Children's self-esteem can be strengthened by parents who blend acceptance with democratic and consistent discipline and by teachers who establish multidimensional classrooms in which many different abilities are valued. The self-esteem of older adults can be increased by reducing their tendency to internalize ageist attitudes.

KEY TERMS

ageism
autonomy versus shame and doubt
categorical self
diffusion status
display rules
foreclosure status
generativity versus stagnation
identity
identity achievement status
identity versus role confusion
industry versus inferiority

initiative versus guilt
integrity versus despair
intimacy versus isolation
life review
looking-glass self
moratorium status
personality
self-concept
self-esteem
social comparison
temperament
trust versus mistrust

334

335

CHAPTER ELEVEN

"Is it a boy (or a girl)?" When proud new parents telephone to announce a birth, that is the first question friends and family tend to ask (Intons-Peterson & Reddel, 1984). It's not long before children know they are girls or boys. Little girls acquire a taste for frilly dresses and dollhouses, while little boys race their toy cars across the carpet or wrestle each other on the lawn. As adults, we never lose our awareness of being either men or women. We define ourselves partly in terms of our "feminine" or "masculine" qualities, and we play roles in keeping with our society's view of what a woman or a man should be. In short, being female or male is a highly important aspect of the self throughout the life span.

In this chapter, we will be looking at how the characteristics and life experiences of male and female humans differ — and why. We will try to determine just how similar and how different males and females are during different periods of the life span. We will see how girls and boys learn to play their parts as girls or boys and how they are groomed for their roles as women or men, and we will consider some of the ways in which adult men and women are steered along different developmental paths in our society. In addition, we will explore an aspect of development that ultimately becomes quite central to our concepts of ourselves as males or females — the development of human sexuality.

MALE AND FEMALE: SORTING OUT THE DIFFERENCES

What are the implications of being a male or a female? We can think in terms of physical differences, psychological differences, and differences in roles played in society. The physical differences are undeniable. A zygote that receives an X chromosome from each parent is a genetic (XX) female, whereas a zygote that receives a Y chromosome from the father is a genetic (XY) male. Chromosomal differences result in different prenatal hormone balances in

males and females, and hormones are responsible for the facts that the genitals of males and females differ and that only females can bear children. Moreover, males typically grow to be taller, heavier, and more muscular than females, while females may be the hardier sex in that they live longer and are less susceptible to many physical disorders. Some theorists argue that biological differences between males and females are ultimately responsible for psychological and social differences between the sexes (for example, that the male hormone testosterone predisposes males to be more aggressive than females). Later in the chapter, we will explore the notion that certain differences between the sexes have a biological basis.

However, there is much more to being male or female than biological heritage. Virtually all societies expect the two sexes to adopt different **gender roles**, the patterns of behavior and traits that define how to act the part of a female or a male in a particular society.[1] Characteristics and behaviors viewed as desirable for males or females are

[1] We use the term *sex* when we are referring to the distinction between biological males and biological females and the term *gender* when we are discussing masculine and feminine traits and behavior patterns that develop as social influences interact with biology. Although many developmentalists speak of *sex roles* or *sex-role stereotypes* where we speak of *gender roles* or *gender-role stereotypes*, we believe that it is useful to emphasize through our use of terms that most differences between the sexes are not purely biological but instead are related to socialization experiences.

336

GENDER ROLES AND SEXUALITY

specified in **gender-role norms** — that is, society's expectations or standards concerning what males and females should be like (Pleck, 1981). Each society's norms generate **gender-role stereotypes**, overgeneralized and largely inaccurate beliefs about what males and females are like (Pleck, 1981). Through the process of **gender typing**, children not only become aware that they are biological males or females but acquire the motives, values, and patterns of behavior that their culture considers appropriate for members of their biological sex. Through the gender-typing process, for example, little Susie might learn a gender-role norm stating that women should strive to be good mothers and gender-role stereotypes indicating that women are more skilled at nurturing children than men are. As an adult, Susan might then adopt the traditional feminine role by quitting her job when her first child is born and devoting herself to the task of mothering.

We would be very mistaken, then, to credit any differences that we observe between girls and boys or women and men to biological causes. They could just as easily be due to differences in the ways in which males and females are perceived and raised. But before we try to explain sex differences, perhaps we should find out what these differences are believed to be and what they actually are.

Gender Norms and Stereotypes

Which sex is more likely to express emotions? to be tidy? to be competitive? to use harsh language? If you are like most people, you undoubtedly have some ideas about how men and women differ psychologically and can easily answer these questions.

The female's role as childbearer is largely responsible for the gender-role norms that have prevailed in our society. Girls have typically been encouraged to assume an **expressive role** that involves being kind, nurturant, cooperative, and sensitive to the needs of others (Parsons, 1955). These psychological traits, it is assumed, will prepare girls to play the roles of wife and mother — to keep the family functioning and to raise children successfully. By contrast, boys have been encouraged to adopt an **instrumental role**, for as a traditionally defined husband and father, the male faces the tasks of providing for the family and protecting it from harm. Thus boys are expected to become dominant, independent, assertive, and competitive. Similar norms for males and females apply in many, though certainly not all, societies. In most nonindustrial societies, for example, boys

are pressured more strongly than girls to become achievement oriented and self-reliant, and girls are more strongly encouraged than boys to become nurturant, responsible, and obedient (Barry, Bacon, & Child, 1957). All of these traits are typically valued in both sexes, but the emphasis placed on each depends on the sex of the child (Zern, 1984).

When cultural norms demand that females play an expressive role and males play an instrumental role, we naturally assume that females actually possess expressive traits and males possess instrumental traits. That is, we form stereotypes of males and females and then make assumptions about what people are like solely on the basis of knowing they are male or female (Broverman, Vogel, Broverman, Clarkson, & Rosenkrantz, 1972). If you are thinking that these stereotypes have disappeared as attention to women's rights has increased and as more women have entered the labor force, you are wrong. Although change has occurred, many adolescents and young adults still endorse many traditional stereotypes about masculinity and femininity and prefer individuals who conform to these stereotypes (Lewin & Tragos, 1987; Ruble, 1983; Shaffer & Johnson, 1980; White, Kruczek, Brown, & White, 1989). Might these notions have a basis in fact, then? Let's see.

Actual Psychological Differences Between the Sexes

In a classic review of more than 1500 studies comparing males and females, Eleanor Maccoby and Carol Jacklin (1974) concluded that only four common gender stereotypes are reasonably accurate (that is, are consistently supported by research):

1. Females have greater **verbal abilities** than males. Girls tend to develop verbal skills at an earlier age than boys, but sex differences are not always clearcut until adolescence, as indicated by measures of such things as vocabulary, reading comprehension, and speech fluency.

2. Males outperform females on tests of **visual/spatial ability** (for example, arranging blocks in patterns, identifying the same figure from different angles). Although Maccoby and Jacklin concluded that these differences emerge only in childhood and then persist across the life span (Linn & Petersen, 1985).

3. Similarly, males outperform females on the average

337

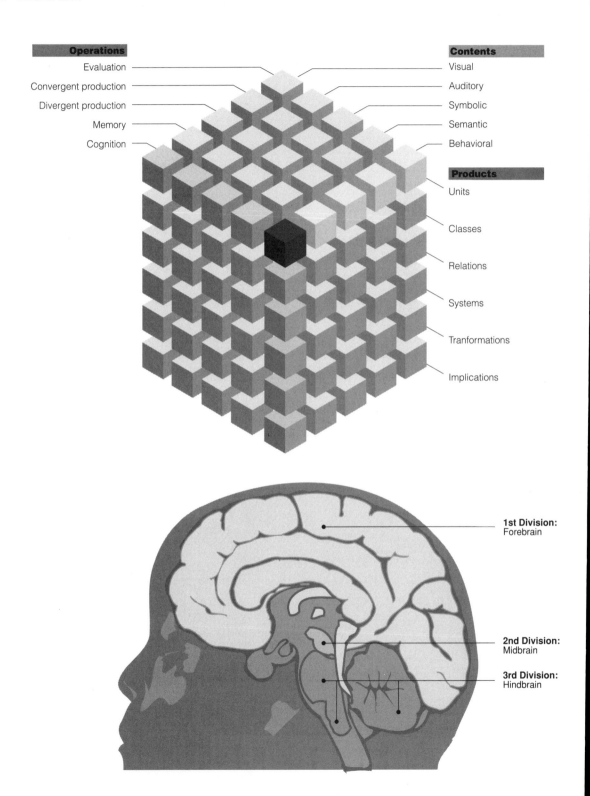

Operations
- Evaluation
- Convergent production
- Divergent production
- Memory
- Cognition

Contents
- Visual
- Auditory
- Symbolic
- Semantic
- Behavioral

Products
- Units
- Classes
- Relations
- Systems
- Tranformations
- Implications

1st Division: Forebrain

2nd Division: Midbrain

3rd Division: Hindbrain

Careful choices of tints can give a lift to otherwise mundane textbook diagrams. While not essential to conveying the educational information, these techniques help guide and motivate the student to learn. At the left, note the orderly line-up of callouts that describe the area of interest. The circular diagram at the bottom of this page uses no lines, just graduated tints to separate the information.

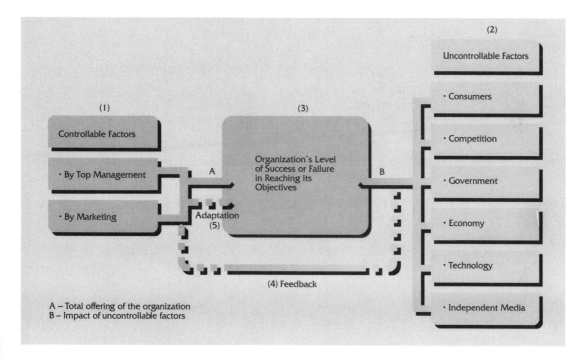

(1) Controllable Factors
· By Top Management
· By Marketing

A

Adaptation (5)

(3) Organization's Level of Success or Failure in Reaching its Objectives

B

(4) Feedback

(2) Uncontrollable Factors
· Consumers
· Competition
· Government
· Economy
· Technology
· Independent Media

A – Total offering of the organization
B – Impact of uncontrollable factors

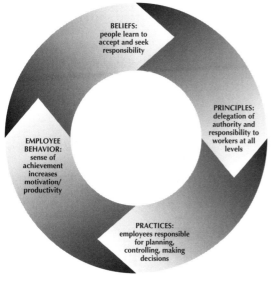

BELIEFS: people learn to accept and seek responsibility

PRINCIPLES: delegation of authority and responsibility to workers at all levels

PRACTICES: employees responsible for planning, controlling, making decisions

EMPLOYEE BEHAVIOR: sense of achievement increases motivation/ productivity

Flow charts
Drop shadows and dynamic shading make these two flow charts more interesting.

This magazine cover uses a large number of typefaces yet maintains readability. Note the many contrasts in size and shape in the various letterforms.

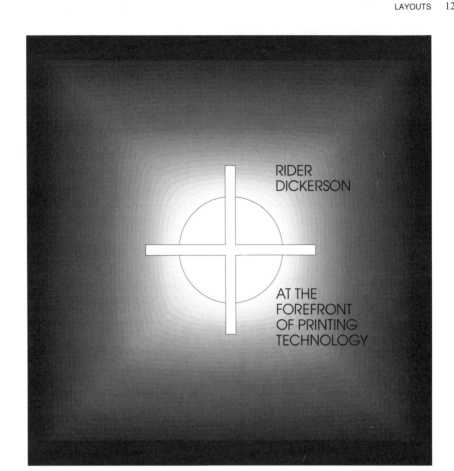

This book cover uses graduated gray to focus the reader's attention on the registration mark in the center.

The project sheet below uses gray as a design element to separate the *eight days* of this company's work week.

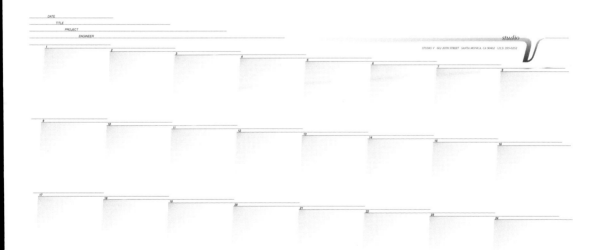

Logos

Black and White

To be most effective at all sizes and methods of reproduction means a logo should stand up well in just black and white. Not dependent on gray screens, patterns or colors, black-and-white logos are versatile and dramatic.

CHARLES WYKE-SMITH
PROGRAM

JOHN ODAM
FREEHAND

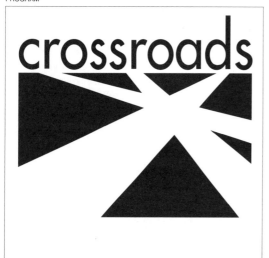

TOM GOULD
FREEHAND

(Opposite, top left) This high-contrast logo uses bold white slashes on a black field to catch the viewer's eye. Note how the "roads" continually lead your eye back to the type. Crisp and lively! (Opposite, top right) The figure for this powerful logo started as a tracing of a photograph. The trace was scanned and autotraced in a PostScript drawing program to achieve the final wood-cut style. The sharp edges and strong black/white contrast suit the revolutionary nature of the subject matter. Note also the use of contrasting bolder type to emphasize the important portion of the name.

(Opposte bottom) This elegant image is composed of three elements: the custom type the illustration of the mountain, and the frame that surrounds them. Notice how the type is set very tight, yet still remains quite readable. In the illustration, there's nice contrast between the curves of the sun, hill, path and bushes and the angular mountain and trees. A beautiful black-and-white symbol—who needs gray?

JOHN ODAM
FREEHAND

ROBERT RUBAYAN
ADOBE ILLUSTRATOR

(Left) This product logo makes a strong visual impression, thanks to the bold Futura type, the two black fields and thick black outlines. The bold vertical format is broken by the word "volley," making the reader view the type first, then look at the graphic. Notice how the aligned vertical stems of the letterforms in the center of the logo serve to connect the two black fields.

(Above right) Calligraphy with the digital touch! Originally hand-inked, a scan of the original was used as a template and traced in a PostScript drawing program.

Black Plus a Tone

Adding one or more gray tones adds to the depth
and richness of the logo. However, it's a good idea
to ask yourself if the grays you are using enhance or
detract from the image.

BERT MONROY
ADOBE ILLUSTRATOR

(Above) This decorative
type solution was
originally hand-drawn,
then scanned and
imported into a PostScript
drawing program. The
scanned image was
traced using bezier
curves, filled with black
and duplicated. The
duplication was filled with
a light gray, offset and
sent behind the original.

(Right) This cut-paper
style of graphic for a
restaurant uses a custom
font and multiple gray
shades. The end result is
totally Californian!

ALLAN MILLER
FREEHAND

JOHN ODAM
FREEHAND

(Left) Custom type (derived from an existing typeface) is the foundation for this logo for an Irish bar. The multiple shades of gray and the interwoven decorative element give this piece a dynamic yet refined appeal.

(Below) The type for this attractive logo type combines a high-tech "digital readout" look with an Oriental calligraphic feel. Note how much more easily the logo reads when the "corp" is in gray. For some projects—if the client's printing budget allows—a second color could replace the gray.

ALLAN MILLER
FREEHAND

JOHN ODAM
FREEHAND

This Art Deco style logo for an event run by the American Institute of Graphic Artists uses the designers' original alphabet. Note how the graduated gray makes the "fun" solid black circles stand out. Also note how the angled, delicate, serif-faced "AIGA" type provides a nice foil for the relatively busy "Technologies."

Graduated Screens

Some programs make it possible to achieve a blend of one gray tone to another. Blending, a dynamic "air-brush" effect with many creative possibilities, should be used cautiously, keeping in mind the type of output you are using. Some very long or complex pathways that are filled with graduated or radial blended tones may give the laser printer and imagesetter some trouble.

CHARLES WYKE-SMITH
FREEHAND

Gentle radial and
graduated fills make
up the water, mountain
and sun/sky for this
attractive logo.

Special-Effect Screens

Coarse half-tone dots and stylish "tiger teeth" zig-zags are another way to get a tonal blend. These screens are suitable for lower quality paper and smaller sizes.

JACK DAVIS
ADOBE ILLUSTRATOR

JACK DAVIS
IMAGESTUDIO/FREEHAND

JOHN ODAM
FREEHAND

(Above left) Another custom font, fittingly designed in old Celtic style, stands at the head of this logo/banner. Overall, the logo shows good light/dark contrast; also notice the nice contrast of the curved waves against the spike-filled ship.

JACK DAVIS
FREEHAND

(Opposite top right) A single, thin diamond shape, repeated, grouped, duplicated and rotated creates this simple but vibrant logo. This mark is even more effective at a smaller size.

(Opposite center right) This symbol was given a large, graduated halftone dot screen in an image retouching program, then imported into a PostScript drawing program. The image was then skewed to the left into a kind of reverse italic.

(Opposite bottom right) A simplified image that says a lot. The eye is first drawn to the high contrast area of the boat sails. The image has been reduced to the bare essentials, a necessity if the symbol is to be widely promoted.

(Right) These clever initials started as scanned type, traced in a PostScript drawing program. The graduated gray background works well with the custom spikes of the letterforms.

(Below right) The two very different yet beautifully effective solutions for an observatory's logo make good use of the computer's ability to create graduated fills. The first example uses a large halftone dot pattern; the second uses a straight line pattern. Note that although there are no grays used, the eye tends to create them from the coarse line screens.

ALLAN MILLER
FREEHAND

TOM GOULD
FREEHAND

Three-Dimensional

Only one of the logos on this page was created in a
3-D program; the others used standard drawing or
painting tools to simulate a 3-D effect.

(Right) These fanciful initial caps—part of an entire alphabet—use black, white and three shades of gray to create a multi-layered effect. Look closely at how the black drop shadow immediately behind the letterforms makes them appear "punched out" of the gray background. The pyramid motif, repeated in different positions with each letter, uses a gray drop shadow to make it "float" above the letter.

(Below left) A logo of contrasts: heavy block shapes seem to float on the page.

(Below right) This 3-D logo (created in a PostScript drawing program) is a study in effective contrasts. The "Update" in light type provides a good foil for the heavy "ACE." The white rule around the "C" separates the tightly kerned letterforms, visually adding another layer to the logo.

DON BAKER
FREEHAND

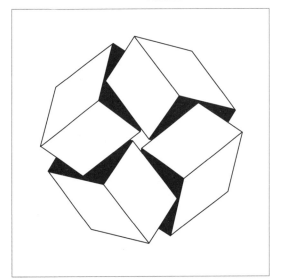

JACK DAVIS
MACDRAW

BERT MONROY
ADOBE ILLUSTRATOR

JACK DAVIS
PHOTOSHOP

(Top right) This logo was created entirely in a photo-retouching/painting program. Note the subtle touches, especially the border around the type.

(Center right) All of the graduated grays in this logo were generated automatically by the 3-D program. The highlights on the bottoms of the letters are an especially nice touch.

(Below right) The theater's original logo was converted to PostScript format and brought into an image-retouching program. Several gray-scale effects were then applied. The final image was used in both print and broadcast media.

JACK DAVIS
SWIVEL 3-D

JACK DAVIS
FREEHAND/PHOTOSHOP

JOHN ODAM
FREEHAND/STRATAVISION

(Above) Encapsulated
PostScript files from
Freehand were placed into
Stratavision, given a
wood-grained surface,
then extruded to create
this 3-D graphic.

(Below) Type created in a
PostScript drawing
program, combined with a
TIFF file (the man's face),
makes this interesting
political statement. Note
how creative use of type
gives a wall-like effect.

Textures

Another way to add spice and flavor to a logo is to experiment with unusual textures and surfaces. Like any strong condiment they should be used with care and caution.

ED ROXBURGH
IMAGESTUDIO

(Top right) The original art was first inked by brush, creating a gray "wash." The art was then scanned and adjusted in an image-retouching program. The end result is very high tech, high touch.

JACK DAVIS/JOHN ODAM
FREEHAND/PHOTOSHOP

(Center right) The original typographic design for this screen image of an interactive multimedia project was created in a PostScript drawing program, then given a relief texture treatment (similar to the embossed initial cap effects in Chapter 3) in an image-retouching program.

(Below right) A 3-D program helped create these avant-garde billiard balls, using a "texture mapping" feature.

Illustrations

This section contains illustrations by talented artists who are experienced with a wide variety of digital illustration tools. The section is organized from the simple to the more complex. The first several pages focus on bitmapped illustration; then the emphasis shifts to PostScript illustration; then scanned images (both bitmapped and gray-scale); and finally to pieces where two or more pieces of software were used to create the final image.

MARTIN SPEED
MACPAINT

The artist used a simple bitmapped painting program to re-create two famous paintings, Dali's *The Persistence of Memory* and Matisse's *Dance*. Note how the consistent use of angled line fills gives continuity to both pieces.

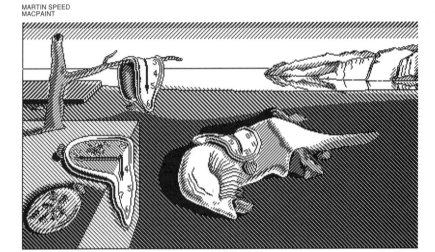

Using standard bitmapped patterns and the spray can and paint brush tools gives this scene a gritty, real-world appearance. The attention to detail is marvelous, especially the effect of the hanging overhead light and the shadows it casts.

BERT MONROY
MACPAINT

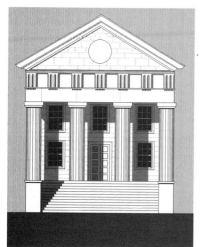

Note the careful use of grays in these architectural forms. In the far left example, the shadows of the columns fall on the building, giving it a 3-D look.

TONY BROWN

BERT MONROY
MACPAINT

(Above) This surreal scene becomes believable through the use of perspective—notice the detail in the parched landscape in the foreground. The shading of objects is also very consistent. The light source is the ominous sun just outside the frame.

(Opposite) This icon-like illustration was created in several layers to achieve the final effect. The light source is above and slightly to the left of the images, throwing the shadow down and to the right. Note the contrast of the white-outlined, hand-drawn Pharaoh with the darker, geometrical pyramid shapes.

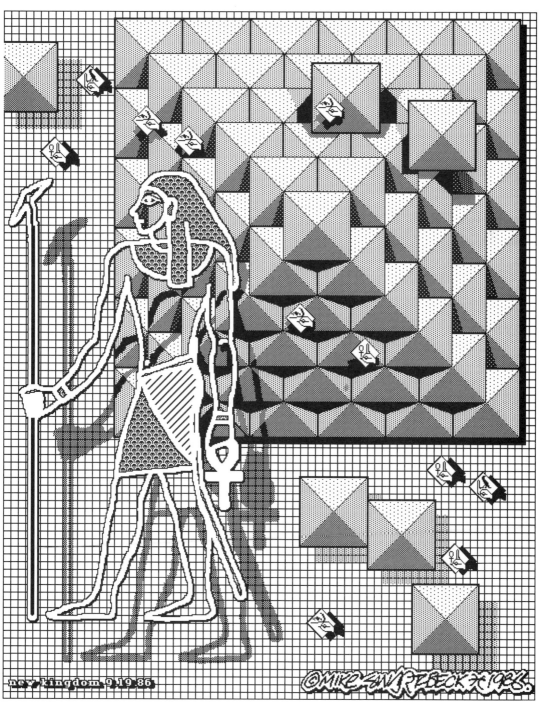

new kingdom 9.19.86

MIKE SWARTZBECK
GRAPHIC WORKS

These fun, cartoonish drawings show a serious use of gray. The graduated tints give shape and fullness to the illustrations.

JUNKO HOSHIGAWA
PIXEL PAINT

Custom patterns
developed in a PostScript
drawing program provide
the basis for these easily
modified dresses. Patterns
that can be changed
quickly are of real benefit
to fashion and gift wrap
designers.

LISA KING
ADOBE ILLUSTRATOR

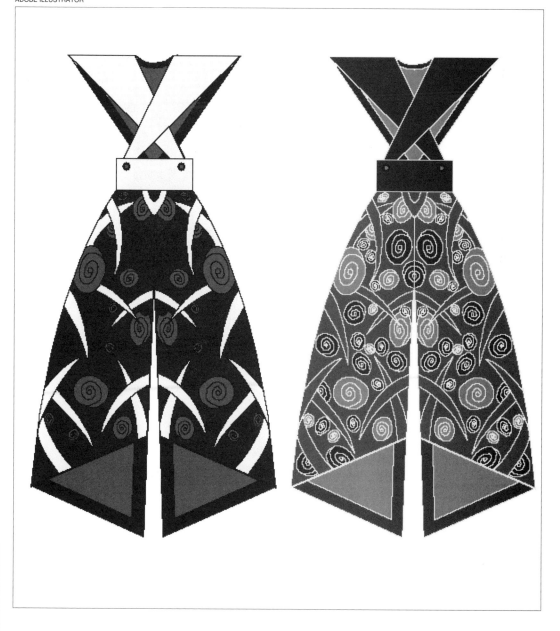

Simple and bold, these illustrations make a statement using strong black-and-white contrast. Saved in PostScript, they can be easily altered to suit your purpose.

Not all clip art is black and white! These nature images show an excellent use of blended grays, giving them a realistic three-dimensional appearance.

CLICK ART CLIP ART
ADOBE
ILLUSTRATOR

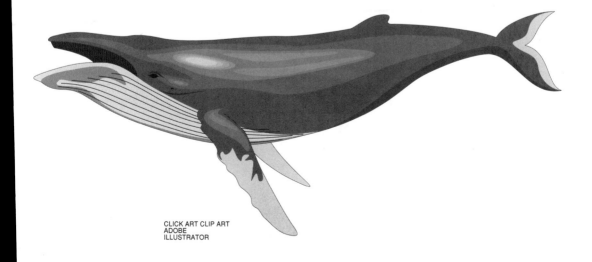

CLICK ART CLIP ART
ADOBE
ILLUSTRATOR

The artist's paper-cut-out style shows masterful use of straight vs. curved, thick vs. thin and, of course, light vs. dark. Gray is used with a painterly effect on the neo-cubist "Music" at the right, while "Font Wars" below modifies and repeats elements to achieve a warlike uniformity.

MAX SEABAUGH
ADOBE ILLUSTRATOR

MAX SEABAUGH
ADOBE ILLUSTRATOR

TOMOYA IKEDA
ADOBE ILLUSTRATOR

(Left) The elegant, organic shapes of this minimalist line drawing suit the subject perfectly. A great example of how less can truly be more!

(Below) An intricate line-art example showing a good straight/curved contrast. Note how subtly different densities are achieved with a single line weight.

TOMOYA IKEDA
ADOBE ILLUSTRATOR

A fanciful combination!
A few minutes spent
examining this piece will
be well rewarded.
Especially noteworthy
are the highlights along
the barrels of the
drafting instruments,
which give them a three-
dimensional look and
make them stand out
amid the flatter 2-D art.

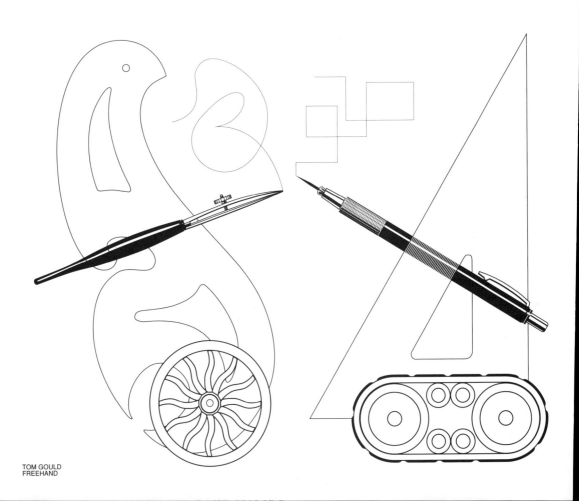

TOM GOULD
FREEHAND

Attention to detail makes
this line art drawing
successful. The eye
follows the direction of the
sail to the deck of the ship,
then back up in roughly a
circular motion.

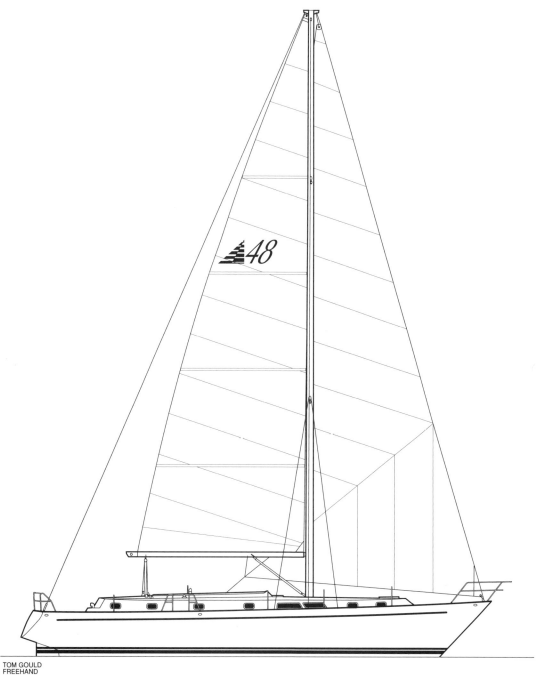

TOM GOULD
FREEHAND

GLENN MITSUI
FREEHAND

A beautifully effective use of black, white and a single gray, this "industrial design" poster uses contrast to get the message across. Note how the use of negative space creates the middle man holding the flag; the high-contrast area where the plane breaks out of the white starburst; the various style contrasts of the letter "A"; and how all the elements are arranged and balanced to keep the eye moving around.

LOUIS FISHAUF
ADOBE ILLUSTRATOR

These playful but powerful images make exceptionally good use of curved vs. straight contrast. Gray is used as a simple accent in "Cubist Head," and as various graduated screen effects in "Dog Woman." The thick white outline on "Dog Woman" makes each of the shapes distinctive.

LOUIS FISHAUF
ADOBE ILLUSTRATOR

(Below) Multiple gray shades and an exaggerated perspective view give this piece a photographic realism.

(Opposite) Another study in contrasts. The white head of the mushroom stands out in stark relief from the darker gray background. Angular grass contrasts nicely with the softer round shapes. A degree of dimension is added by the mushroom head "breaking out" of the black frame. Nicely done!

BERT MONROY
ADOBE ILLUSTRATOR

Bert Monroy

BERT MONROY
ADOBE ILLUSTRATOR

DON BAKER
FREEHAND

(Opposite) This stunning graphic image uses the computer to create the increasingly popular cut-paper look. The blade-like triangle shapes give the piece vibrancy and a sense of motion.

(Right) Subtle graduated grays give dimension to these icon-like pieces. The angular and tilted forms make the illustrations appear unstable, ready to slide and fall at a moment's notice. The smaller "Coffee Cup" shows how a significant size reduction doesn't affect the quality or impact of the illustration.

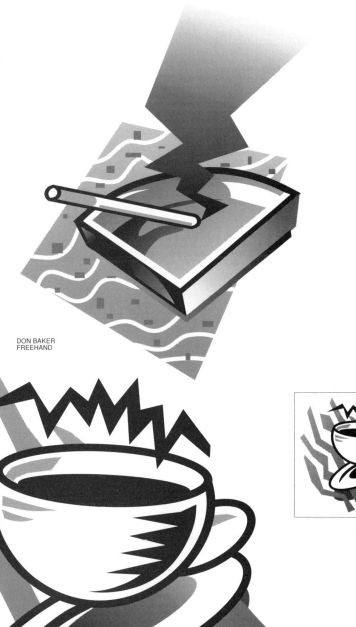

DON BAKER
FREEHAND

TOM GOULD
FREEHAND

Flashback to "op art" of
the 60's! Spend some time
examining these vibrating
images and notice how
they use coarse line
screens to achieve
shading and depth.

TOM GOULD
FREEHAND

JOHN ODAM
ADOBE ILLUSTRATOR
FROM SCANNED TEMPLATE

The "autotrace" feature of many drawing programs can be used to create a "painterly" look. The original artwork of the sun was scanned and used as a template in a PostScript drawing program, then autotraced to achieve a rough, textured appearance.

DEBORAH IVANOFF
FREEHAND

DEBORAH IVANOFF
FREEHAND

Careful examination of
the use of gray on these
game panels will reveal
several nifty techniques
for creating 3-D graphics
in a 2-D program.

This amazingly life-like microcassette recorder contains no graduated grays—a brilliant use of straight gray shades.

BERT MONROY
ADOBE ILLUSTRATOR

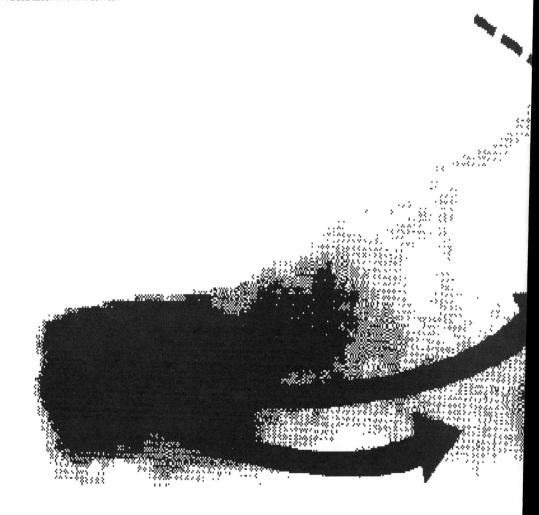

JACK DAVIS
ADOBE ILLUSTRATOR/TYPESTYLER

MIKE URISS
IMAGESTUDIO, ADOBE ILLUSTRATOR

(Opposite) The type within the glasses was created in a type-manipulation program, giving it a "spherized" look. That image was brought into a PostScript drawing program and placed inside the glasses. Note how the black/white contrast makes a powerful impact.

(Below) A posterized TIFF image was brought into a PostScript drawing program. The artist then added the arrows and lines, providing good editorial contrast. (This piece was used for an article on computer-aided design.)

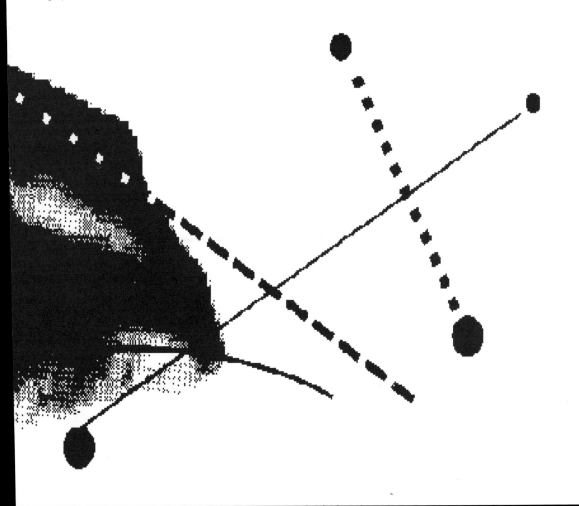

A paint-like image of a traditional painter's tool. The full range of grays is being used here. The light source appears to be from the upper left.

DIANE MARGOLIN
IMAGESTUDIO

This plaque is a study in gray textures: the crocodile-texture border, the burlap-texture letters and the watercolor-like drop shadow. Notice how the subtle highlights on the border give it a third dimension.

ROBERT RUBYAN
IMAGESTUDIO

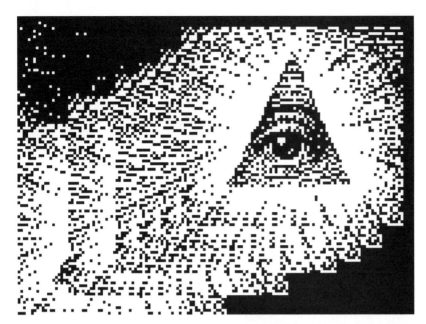

(Above) A scan of a dollar bill was the first step for this piece. The image was then enlarged and modified in a paint program. The repeated background causes the image to move forward toward the viewer.

(Below) Another example of a simple yet effective use of scanned, bitmapped images. The scanner's software was used to posterize this photo, and the eye was duplicated and stretched in a painting program.

MICHAEL GOSNEY
THUNDERSCAN, MACPAINT

(Left) This low-resolution scan from a video camera illustrates an interesting possibility: moving the camera during the scan, creating a sense of motion in the finished piece.

(Below) The eyes have it! The original photo was scanned; the right eye was duplicated, reversed, enlarged, duplicated again and stretched, and so on. The exaggerated, bitmapped look of the eye is a good contrast to the detailed head.

MICHAEL GOSNEY

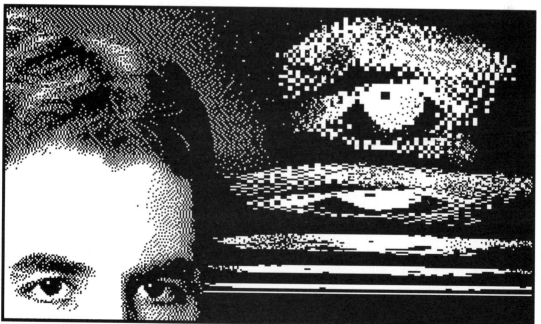

MICHAEL GOSNEY

These illustrations show an effective use of the video camera as a means of capturing images. At the right, "Get Duck" was hand drawn, video scanned, printed out and re-scanned to achieve the desired texture.

Below is a video scan of the artist kissing a drawing.

PAUL RUTOVSKY
MACVISION, FULLPAINT

Rutkovsky 1987

PAUL RUTOVSKY
MACVISION, FULLPAINT

Playing with gray is fun!
The top image combines
a scan with hand-drawn
images to good effect,
while the bottom
example contains all
hand-drawn art.

PAM HOBBS
SUPERPAINT

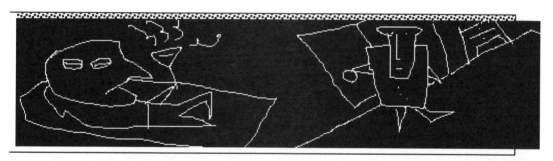

PAM HOBBS
SUPERPAINT

mad dogs and   english   men,

stay out
in the

mid day
sun.

pamela Hobbs © 1989

pam-la.

PAM HOBBS
MACPAINT

(Left) Repetition for effect. One of the group has been enlarged and distorted to add interest to the random pattern.

(Opposite) Multiple layers were used to create this masterpiece of ghostlike transparent effects. Note, for instance, how the forward leg of the dark figure gradually dissolves through the "m."

©MIKE SWARTZBECK · 1988

in dreams alone 12.27

MIKE SWARTZBECK
GRAPHIC WORKS

MIKE SWARTZBECK
MACVISION, MACPAINT

(Above) The bird is a straight video scan; the patterns below are video scans adjusted in a painting program. The patterns—taken from old books—can be used as backgrounds.

© Mike Swartzbeck 1988

MIKE SWARTZBECK
GRAPHIC WORKS

Two images blended
masterfully together
create an exquisite,
memorable montage.

DAVID BRUNN
MACVISION. MACPAINT

(Right) An unaltered video scan of a house and snow-covered ground.

(Below) A video scan of two different photos, modified and combined in a paint program.

(Opposite) Video scans of several images, combined and modified in a gray-scale image retouching program. Note the combination of hard and soft textures.

DAVID BRUNN
MACVISION, MACPAINT

DAVID BRUNN
MACVISION, IMAGESTUDIO

STEPHEN KING
SUPERPAINT, ADOBE ILLUSTRATOR,
IMAGESTUDIO

(Left) An excellent example of a hand-drawn look achieved on the computer. The original art was created in a PostScript drawing program (from a scan) and then imported into a painting program to give it a rough-textured look. The resulting image was brought into a gray-scale retouching program, and the drop shadow was added.

(Opposite) The original sparrow was created in a drawing program, then imported into an image-retouching program to create the embossed look.

JACK DAVIS
MACDRAW, IMAGESTUDIO

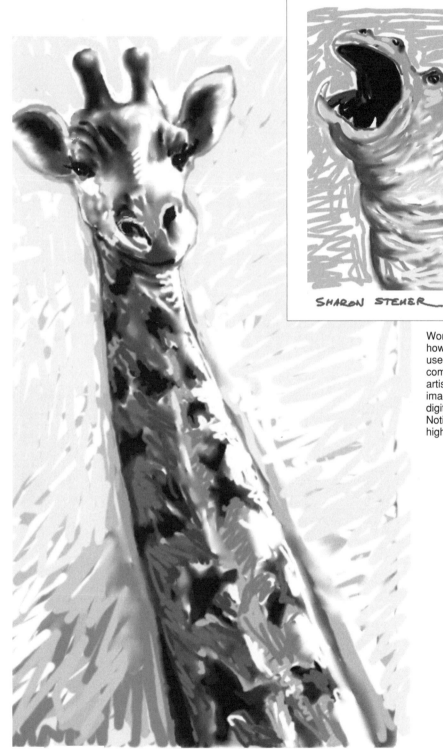

SHARON STEUER

Wonderful examples of
how the computer can be
used to create non-
computer-looking art. The
artist drew each of these
images freehand using a
digitizing tablet and stylus.
Notice the shading and
highlights on each piece.

SHARON STEUER
IMAGESTUDIO

NIRA
DIGITAL DARKROOM

A photo retouching/
painting program was
used to create this high-
quality gray-scale image.
A good example of a
painterly use of
chiaroscuro.

MIKE URISS
IMAGESTUDIO

A showcase of gray
effects. Note how each of
the four panels uses a
distinctly different look.

Photomontage, or the
combining of several
photographic images, can
produce dynamic,
interesting compositions.
Here the artist uses scans
of several found objects to
achieve the desired look.

BRIAN TAYLOR
IMAGESTUDIO

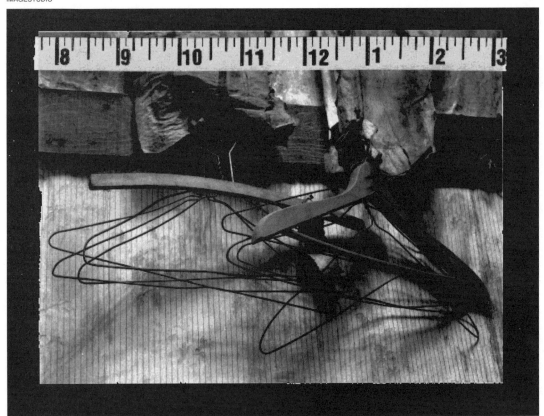

BRIAN TAYLOR
IMAGESTUDIO

DAVID HERROLD
DIGITAL DARKROOM/THUNDERSCAN

Two more examples of
unusual photomontage.
The artist used scans of
photos he had taken over
several years and
combined them in a photo-
retouching program to
create a visual narrative.

JACK DAVIS
IMAGESTUDIO

JACK DAVIS
IMAGESTUDIO

(Above) Many photo retouching programs offer embossing capabilities. Note the subtle texture enhancements created with the program's embossing feature.

(Left) The photo of the couple is a stock photo from the 50's; the magazine is a mock-up that was video scanned. Both were arranged in an image-retouching program for the final effect.

JACK DAVIS
HYPERCARD

Creative use of gray patterns and textures has found its way into the world of multimedia. These samples, taken from an interactive multimedia stack, use textures to distinguish the different categories. Notice how the textures are occasionally lightened to make the text more readable. Also note the attractive, comprehensible 3-D gray icons in the bottom example.

Three-dimensional clip art offers versatile, interesting graphics that may be modified with relative ease. Each of these examples has two light sources.

SWIVEL 3D
CLIP ART

SWIVEL 3D
CLIP ART

SWIVEL 3D
CLIP ART

SWIVEL 3D
CLIP ART

JACK DAVIS
ADOBE ILLUSTRATOR, SWIVEL 3-D

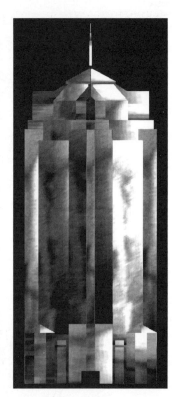

(Top right) Two distinctly different versions of the same building. The version on the left gets an Art Deco treatment in a drawing program, while the 3-D version uses a vivid marble texture.

(Below right) Combining simple shapes in unexpected ways can create surreal results, as this image shows.

(Opposite) The graduated screen backdrop for these 3-D "molecules" makes them appear to float in space.

JACK DAVIS
SWIVEL 3-D

JACK DAVIS
SWIVEL 3-D, ADOBE PHOTOSHOP

Appendix

The Gray Book Appendix lists software and hardware products and useful reference materials.

Software product categories, for Macintosh, MS-DOS and Amiga systems, include Paint, Image-Processing, 3D and Page Layout programs, as well as Clip Art, Templates and Fonts, Font-Design and Font-Manipulation, Utilities and System software. Hardware product categories are Graphic Tablets, Scanners and Digitizers, Monitors, Color Calibration, Storage Systems, Printers and Imagesetters, Large Format Output Services, and Film Recorders. Under references you will find informative periodicals, books and electronic bulletin board services.

We hope these listings will help you find the products and information you need to make the most of your personal computer graphics system.

SOFTWARE

Paint Programs

Color MacCheese
Delta Tao Software
760 Howard Avenue
Sunnyvale, CA 94087
408-730-9336

DeluxePaint 3.0
Electronic Arts
1820 Gateway Drive
San Mateo, CA 94404
415-571-7171

DigiPaint
NewTek
115 W. Crane Street
Topeka, KS 66603
800-843-8934

LaserPaint
LaserWare
PO Box 668
San Rafael, CA 94915
800-367-6898

MacPaint
Claris
440 Clyde Avenue
Mountain View, CA 94043
415-962-8946

PC Paintbrush IV Plus
ZSoft
450 Franklin Road, #100
Marietta, GA 30067
404-428-0008

PixelPaint 2.0
PixelPaint Professional
SuperMac Technology
485 Potrero Avenue
Sunnyvale, CA 94086
408-245-0022

Studio/8
Studio/32
Electronic Arts
1820 Gateway Drive
San Mateo, CA 94404
415-571-7171

SuperPaint 2.0
Silicon Beach Software
9770 Carroll Center Road, Suite J
San Diego, CA 92126
619-695-6956

UltraPaint
Deneba Software
7855 N.W. 12th Street
Miami, FL 33126
800-622-6827

VideoPaint
Olduvai
7520 Red Road, Suite A
South Miami, FL 33143
305-665-4665

Image-Processing

ColorStudio
Digital Darkroom
Silicon Beach Software
9770 Carroll Center Road, Suite J
San Diego, CA 92126
619-695-6956

ImageStudio
Letraset USA
40 Eisenhower Drive
Paramus, NJ 07653
201-845-6100

PhotoMac
Data Translation
100 Locke Drive
Malboro, MA 01752
508-481-3700

Photoshop
Adobe Systems
PO Box 7900
Mountain View, CA 94039-7900
800-344-8335

Picture Publisher
Astral Development
Londonderry Square, Suite 112
Londonderry, NH 03053
603-432-6800

3D Programs

MacRenderMan
Pixar
3240 Kerner Boulevard
San Rafael, CA 94901
415-258-8100

MacroMind 3D
MacroMind
410 Townsend Avenue, Suite 408
San Francisco, CA 94107
415-442-0200

StrataVision 3D
Strata
2 W. Saint George Boulevard
Ancestor Square, Suite 2100
St. George, UT 84770
801-628-5218

Super 3D
Silicon Beach Software
9770 Carroll Center Road, Suite J
San Diego, CA 92126
619-695-6956

Swivel 3D
Paracomp
1725 Montgomery Street, Second Floor
San Francisco, CA 94111
415-956-4091

Zing
Mindscape
3444 Dundee Road, Suite 203
Northbrook, IL 60062
708-480-7667

PostScript Illustration Software

Adobe Illustrator
Adobe Systems
PO Box 7900
Mountain View, CA 94039-7900
800-344-8335

Aldus FreeHand
Aldus
411 First Avenue S.
Seattle, WA 98104
206-622-5500

Arts & Letters
Computer Support
15926 Midway Road
Dallas, TX 75244
214-661-8960

Corel Draw
Corel Systems
1600 Carling Avenue, Suite 190
Ottawa, ON K1Z 8R7 Canada
613-728-8200

Cricket Draw
Cricket Software
40 Valley Stream Parkway
Mallvern, PA 19355
215-251-9890

Cricket Stylist
Computer Associates
10505 Sorrento Valley Road
San Diego, CA 92121-1698
619-452-0170

GEM Artline
Digital Research
70 Garden Court
Monterey, CA 93940
408-649-3896

Micrografx Designer
Micrografx
1303 Arapaho Road
Richardson, TX 75081-1769
800-272-3729

Smart Art, Volumes I, II, III
Emerald City Software
1040 Marsh Road, Suite 110
Menlo Park, CA 94025
415-324-8080

Streamline
Adobe Systems
PO Box 7900
Mountain View, CA 94039-7900
800-344-8335

Draw Programs

Canvas 2.0
Deneba Software
7855 N.W. 12th Street
Miami, FL 33126
800-622-6827

MacDraw 2.0
Claris
440 Clyde Avenue
Mountain View, CA 94043
415-962-8946

Page Layout Programs

DesignStudio
Letraset USA
40 Eisenhower Drive
Paramus, NJ 07653
201-845-6100

FrameMaker
Frame Technology
1010 Rincon Circle
San Jose, CA 95131
408-433-1928

PageMaker
Aldus
411 First Avenue S.
Seattle, WA 98104
206-622-5500

Personal Press
Silicon Beach Software
9770 Carroll Center Road, Suite J
San Diego, CA 92126
619-695-6956

QuarkXPress
Quark
300 S. Jackson Street, Suite 100
Denver, CO 80209
800-543-7711

Qura Publisher
Xerox Product Support
1301 Ridgeview Drive
Lewisville, TX 75067
800-822-8221

Prepress Systems

Aldus PrePrint
Aldus
411 First Avenue S.
Seattle, WA 98104
206-622-5500

ArtClips
Tactic Software
13615 South Dixie Highway, Suite 118
Miami, FL 33176
305-378-4110

Art Nouveau Images
Silicon Designs
PO Box 2234
Orinda, CA 94563-6634
415-254-1460

Clip Art for Ministry
The Church Art Works
875 High Street, N.E.
Salem, OR 97301
503-370-9377

Crosfield
Crosfield Systems
65 Harristown Road
Glen Rock, NJ 07452
201-447-5800, ext. 5310

Flash Graphics
Flash Graphics
PO Box 1950
Sausalito, CA 94965
415-331-7700

Freedom of Press
Custom Applications
900 Technology Park Drive, Bldg. 8
Billerica, MA 01821
508-667-8585

Illustrated Art Backgrounds
ARTfactory
414 Tennessee Plaza, Suite A
Redlands, CA 92373
714-793-7346

Images with Impact
3G Graphics
11410 N.E. 124th Street, Suite 6155
Kirkland, WA 98034
206-823-8198

Lightspeed Color Layout System
Lightspeed
47 Farnsworth Street
Boston, MA 02210
617-338-2173

Metro ImageBase Electronic Art
Metro ImageBase
18623 Ventura Boulevard, Suite 210
Tarzana, CA 91356
800-525-1552

Moonlight Art Works
Hired Hand Design
3608 Faust Avenue
Long Beach, CA 90808
213-429-2936

Photo Gallery
NEC Technologies
1414 Massachusetts Avenue
Boxborough, MA 01719
508-264-8000

PicturePaks
Marketing Graphics
4401 Dominion Boulevard, Suite 210
Glen Allen, VA 23060
804-747-6991

Printware 720 IQ Laser Imager
Printware
1385 Mendota Heights Road
Saint Paul, MN 55120
612-456-1400

Pro-Art Professional
Art Library Trilogy 1
Multi-Ad Services
1720 W. Detweiller Drive
Peoria, Il 61615
309-692-11530

Professional Photography Collection
discImagery
18 E. 16th Street
New York, NY 10003
212-675-8500

PS Portfolio, Spellbinder Art Library
Lexisoft
PO Box 5000
Davis, CA 95617-5000
916-758-3630

The Right Images
Tsunami Press
275 Route 18
East Brunswick, NJ 08816
800-448-9815

SpectreSeps PM
Pre-Press Technologies
2441 Impala Drive
Carlsbad, CA 92008
619-931-2695

TextArt
Stone Design
2425 Teodoro N.W.
Albuquerque, NM 87107
505-345-4800

Totem Graphics
Totem Graphics
5109-A Capitol Boulevard
Tumwater, WA 98501
206-352-1851

Type Foundry
U-Design
201 Ann Street
Hartford, CT 06102
203-278-3648

Visionary
Scitex America
8 Oak Park Drive
Bedford, MA 01730
617-275-5150

Vivid Impressions
Casady & Greene
26080 Carmel Rancho Boulevard
Suite 202
Carmel, CA 93923
800-359-4920

Works of Art
Springboard Software
7808 Creekridge Circle
Minneapolis, MN 55435
612-944-3915

Templates

Desktop Manager Style Sheets
New Riders Publishing
31125 Via Colinas, Suite 902
Westlake Village, CA 91362
818-991-5392

Document Gallery Style Sheets
Micro Publishing
21150 Hawthorne Boulevard, Suite 104
Torrance, CA 90503
213-371-5787

Layouts
Starburst Designs
1973 N. Nellis Boulevard, Suite 315
Las Vegas, NV 89115
702-453-3371

Page Designs Quick
Par Publishing
6355 Topanga Canyon Boulevard
Suite 307
Woodland Hills, CA 91367
818-340-8165

PageMaker Portfolio Series
Aldus Corporation
411 First Avenue S.
Seattle, WA 98104
206-622-5500

QuarkStyle
Quark
300 S. Jackson Street, Suite100
Denver, CO 80209
800-356-9363

Will-Harris Designer Disks
Daniel Will-Harris, Dept. M
PO Box 480265
Los Angeles, CA 90048

Fonts

Adobe Type Library
Adobe Systems, Inc.
PO Box 7900
Mountain View, CA 94039-7900
800-344-8335

**Bitstream fonts and
Fontware Installation Kit**
Bitstream
215 First Street
Cambridge, MA 02142
800-522-3668

CG Type
Agfa Compugraphic Division
90 Industrial Way
Wilmington, MA 01887
800-622-8973

**Corel Headline, Corel Loader,
Corel Newfont**
Corel Systems
1600 Carling Avenue, Suite 190
Ottawa, ON K1Z 8R7 Canada
613-728-8200

18+ Fonts
18+ Fonts
337 White Hall Terrace
Bloomingdale, IL 60108
312-980-0887

Em Dash fonts
Em Dash
PO Box 8256
Northfield, IL 60093
312-441-6699

Emigre Fonts
Emigre
48 Shattuck Square, Suite 175
Berkeley, CA 94704-1140

Fluent Laser Fonts
Casady & Greene
26080 Carmel Rancho Boulevard
Suite 202
Carmel, CA 93923
800-359-4920

Font Factory Fonts (for LaserJet)
The Font Factory
13601 Preston Road, Suite 500-W
Dallas, TX 75240
214-239-6085

FontGen IV Plus
VS Software
PO Box 165920
Little Rock, AR 72216
501-376-2083

Font Solution Pack
SoftCraft
16 N. Carroll Street, Suite 500
Madison, WI 53073
608-257-3300

**Hewlett-Packard Soft Fonts
(for LaserJet)**
Hewlett-Packard
PO Box 60008
Sunnyvale, CA 94088-60008
800-538-8787

Hot Type
Image Club Graphics
1902 11th Street S.E.
Calgary, AB T2G 3G2 Canada
800-661-9410

Kingsley/ATF typefaces
(ATF Classic type)
Type Corporation
2559-2 E. Broadway
Tucson, AZ 85716
800-289-8973

Laser fonts and font utilities
SoftCraft
16 N. Carroll Street, Suite 500
Madison, WI 53703
800-351-0500

Laserfonts
Century Software/MacTography
326-D N. Stonestreet Avenue
Rockville, MD 20850
301-424-1357

Monotype fonts
Monotype Typography
53 W. Jackson Boulevard, Suite 504
Chicago, IL 60604
800-666-6897

Ornate Typefaces
Ingrimayne Software
PO Box 404
Rensselaer, IN 47978
219-866-6241

Typographic Ornaments
The Underground Grammarian
PO Box 203
Glassboro, NJ 08028
609-589-6477

URW fonts
The Font Company
12629 N. Tatum Boulevard, Suite 210
Phoenix, AZ 85032
800-442-3668

Varityper fonts
Tegra/Varityper
11 Mt. Pleasant Avenue
East Hanover, NJ 07936
201-884-6277

VS Library of Fonts
VS Software
PO Box 165920
Little Rock, AR 72216
501-376-2083

Font-Design and Font-Manipulation Software

Art Importer
Family Builder
Fontographer
Altsys
720 Avenue F, Suite 109
Plano, TX 75074
214-424-4888

FontLiner
Taylored Graphics
PO Box 1900
Freedom, CA 95019
408-761-2481

FontMaker
The Font Factory
13601 Preston Road, Suite 500 W.
Dallas, TX 75240
214-239-6085

FontSizer
U.S. Microlabs
1611 Headway Circle, Bldg. 3
Austin, TX 78754
512-339-0001

FontStudio
LetraStudio and LetraFont Library
Letraset USA
40 Eisenhower Drive
Paramus, NJ 07653
201-845-6100

LetrTuck
EDCO Services
12410 N. Dale Mabry Hwy.
Tampa, FL 33618
813-962-7800

Pairs Professional Kerning Editor
and Kerning Tables
Pairs Software
160 Vaderhoff Avenue, Suite 201
Toronto, Ontario, Canada, M4G 4B8
416-467-81978

Publisher's Type Foundry
ZSoft
450 Franklin Road, #100
Marietta, GA 30067
404-428-0008

Type Align
Emerald City Software
PO Box 2103
Menlo Park, CA 94026
415-324-8080

Type Director
Hewlett-Packard
3000 Hanover Street
Palo Alto, CA 94303-0890
415-857-1501

TypeStyler
Broderbund Software
17 Paul Drive
San Rafael, CA 94903-2101
415-492-3200

Utilities, Desk Accessories and INITs

Adobe Type Manager
Adobe Systems
PO Box 7900
Mountain View, CA 94039-7900
800-344-8335

After Dark screen saver
Berkeley Systems
1700 Shattuck Avenue
Berkeley, CA 94709
415-540-5535

DiskTools Plus
Electronic Arts
1820 Gateway Drive
San Mateo, CA 94404
800-245-4525

Exposure
Preferred Publishers
5100 Poplar Avenue, Suite 706
Memphis, TN 38137
901-683-3383

Flowfazer screen saver
Utopia Grokware
300 Valley Street, Suite 204
Sausalito, CA 94965
415-331-0714

Font/DA Juggler Plus
Alsoft
PO Box 927
Spring, TX 77383-0929
713-353-4090

Kodak Colorsqueeze
Kodak
343 State Street
Rochester, NY 14650
800-233-1650

New Fountain
David Blatner, Parallax Productions
5001 Ravenna Avenue N.E., Suite 13
Seattle, WA 98105

On Cue
Icom Simulations
648 S. Wheeling Road
Wheeling, IL 60090
708-520-4440

Overwood 2.0, shareware
Jim Donnelly, College of Education
University of Maryland
College Park, MD 20742

QuicKeys
CE Software
PO Box 65580
W. Des Moines, IA 50265
515-224-1995

Screen-to-PICT, public domain
Educorp
531 Stevens Avenue, Suite B
Solana Beach, CA 92075
800-843-9497

SmartScrap
Solutions International
30 Commerce Street
Williston, VT 05495
802-658-5506

Suitcase II
Fifth Generation Systems
10049 N. Reiger Road
Baton Rouge, LA 70809
800-873-4384

Communication Software

Microphone II
Software Ventures
2907 Claremont Avenue, Suite 220
Berkeley, CA 94705
800-336-6477

Red Ryder
Free Soft
150 Hickory Drive
Beaver Falls, PA 15010
412-846-2700

HARDWARE

Graphic Tablets

Kurta Graphic Tablets
Kurta
3007 E. Chambers
Phoenix, AZ 85040
602-276-5533

Summagraphics
Summagraphics
325 Heights Road
Houston, TX 77007
713-869-7009

Wacom Digitizing Tablets
Wacom
West 115 Century Road
Paramus, NJ 07652
201-265-4226

Scanners and Digitizers

Abaton Scan 300/FB and 300/S
Abaton Technology
48431 Milmont Drive
Fremont, CA 94538
415-683-2226

Apple Scanner
Apple Computer
20525 Mariani Avenue
Cupertino, CA 95014
408-996-1010

Dest PC Scan 1000 and 2000 series
Dest
1201 Cadillac Court
Milpitas, CA 95035
408-946-7100

DigiView
NewTek
115 W. Crane Street
Topeka, KS 66603
800-843-8934

Howtek ScanMaster II
Howtek
21 Park Avenue
Hudson, NH 03051
603-882-5200

HP ScanJet Plus
Hewlett-Packard
700 71st Avenue
Greeley, CO 80634
303-845-4045

JX-300 and JX-450 Color Scanners
Sharp Electronics
Sharp Plaza, Box C Systems
Mahwah, NJ 07430
201-529-8200

MacVision 2.0
Koala Technologies
70 N. Second Street
San Jose, CA 95113
408-438-0946

Microtek Scanners
Microtek Labs
16901 S. Western Avenue
Gardena, CA 90247
213-321-2121

ProViz Digitizers
Pixelogic
800 W. Cummings Park, Suite 2900
Woburn, MA 01801
617-938-7711

Silverscanner
La Cie
19552 S.W. 90th Court
Tualatin, OR 97062
800-999-0143

ThunderScan
Thunderware
21 Orinda Way
Orinda, CA 94563
415-254-6581

Monitors

Amdek Corporation
3471 N. First Street
San Jose, CA 95134
800-722-6335

Apple Computer
20525 Mariani Avenue
Cupertino, CA 95014
408-996-1010

E-Machines
9305 S.W. Gemini Drive
Beaverton, OR 97005
503-646-6699

MegaGraphics
439 Calle San Pablo
Camarillo, CA 93010
805-484-3799

Mitsubishi Electronics
991 Knox Street
Torrance, CA 90502
213-217-5732

Moniterm Corporation
5740 Green Circle Drive
Minnetonka, MN 55343
612-935-4151

Nutmeg Systems
25 South Avenue
New Canaan, CT 06840
800-777-8439

Radius
1710 Fortune Drive
San Jose, CA 95131
408-434-1010

RasterOps Corporation
2500 Walsh Avenue
Santa Clara, CA 95051
408-562-4200

SuperMac Technology
485 Portrero Avenue
Sunnyvale, CA 94086
408-245-0022

Color Calibration

The Calibrator
Barco
1500 Wilson Way, Suite 250
Smyrna, GA 30082
404-432-2346

PrecisionColor Calibrator
Radius
1710 Fortune Drive
San Jose, CA 95131
408-434-1010

TekColor
Visual Systems Group
5770 Ruffin Road
San Diego, CA 92123
619-292-7330

Storage Systems

Ehman Engineering
97 S. Red Willow Road
Evanston, WY 82930
800-257-1666

Mass Micro Systems
550 Del Ray Avenue
Sunnyvale, CA 94086
800-522-7979

SuperMac Technology
485 Portrero Avenue
Sunnyvale, CA 94086
408-245-2202

Printers and Imagesetters

4CAST
Du Pont Electronic Imaging Systems
300 Bellevue Parkway, Suite 390
Wilmington, DE 19809
800-654-4567

4693D Color Image Printer
Tektronix, Graphics Printing & Imaging Division
PO Box 500, M/S 50-662
Beaverton, OR 97077
503-627-1497

BirmySetter 300 & 400 Imagesetters
Birmy Graphics
PO Box 42-0591
Miami, FL 33142
305-633-3321

CG 9600/9700-PS Imagesetters
Agfa Compugraphic
90 Industrial Way
Wilmington, MA 01887
800-622-8973

Chelgraph A3 Imageprinter
Chelgraph IBX Imagesetter
Electra Products
1 Survey Circle
N. Billerica, MA 01862
508-663-4366

ColorQuick Ink Jet Printer
Tektronix
Graphics Printing & Imaging Division
PO Box 500, M/S 50-662
Beaverton, OR 97077
503-627-1497

Colorsetter 2000
Optronics, an Intergraph Division
7 Stuart Road
Chelmsford, MA 01824
508-256-4511

Compugraphic Imagesetters
Agfa Compugraphic
200 Ballardvale Street
Wilmington, MA 01887
508-658-5600

CrystalPrint Publisher laser printer
Qume
500 Yosemite Drive
Milpitas, CA 95035
800-223-2479

DeskWriter
HP LaserJet Series II
HP PaintJet Ink Jet Printer
Hewlett-Packard
PO Box 60008
Sunnyvale, CA 94088-60008
800-538-8787

GoScript
LaserGo
9235 Trade Place, Suite A
San Diego, CA 92121
619-530-2400

ImageWriter II
LaserWriter II family of printers
Apple Computer, Inc.
20525 Mariani Avenue
Cupertino, CA 95014
408-996-1010

JLaser CR1
Tall Tree Systems
2585 Bayshore Road
Palo Alto, CA 94303
415-493-1980

Lasersmith PS-415 Laser Printers
Lasersmith, Inc.
430 Martin Avenue
Santa Clara, CA 95050
408-727-7700

Linotronic Imagesetters

LZR Series Laser Printers
Dataproducts
6200 Canoga Avenue
Woodland Hills, CA 91365
818-887-8000

Mitsubishi G330-70
color thermal printer
Mitsubishi Electronics America
Computer Peripherals Products
991 Knox Street
Torrance, CA 90502
213-515-3993

Omnilaser Series 2000
Texas Instruments
12501 Research Drive
Austin, TX 78769
512-250-7111

Pacific Page
(PostScript emulation cartridge)
Golden Eagle Micro
8515 Zionsville Road
Indianapolis, IN 46268
317-879-9696

Phaser Color Image Printer
Tektronix, Graphics Printing & Imaging Division
PO Box 500, M/S 50-662
Beaverton, OR 97077
503-627-1497

QMS ColorScript printers
QMS-PS Series Laser Printers
QMS
1 Magnum Pass
Mobile, AL 36618
800-631-2693

Series 1000 Imagesetters
Linotype Company
4215 Oser Avenue
Hauppauge, NY 11788
516-434-2014

Turbo PS Series Laser Printer
NewGen Systems
17580 Newhope Street
Fountain Valley, CA 92708
714-641-2800

UltreSetter
Ultre
145 Pinelawn Road
Melville, NY 11747
516-753-4800

Varityper printers
Varityper, a Tegra Company
11 Mt. Pleasant Avenue
East Hanover, NJ 07936
201-884-6277

Large-Format Output Services

Computer Image Systems
20030 Normandie Avenue
Torrance, CA 90502
800-736-5105

Gamma One
12 Corporate Drive
North Haven, CT 06473
203-234-0440

Jetgraphix
1531 Pontus Avenue, Suite 300
Los Angeles, CA 90025
213-479-4994

Film Recorders

Agfa-Matrix Film Recorder
Agfa
1 Ramland Road
Orangeburg, NY 10962
914-365-0190

FilmPrinter Plus
Mirus
4301 Great America Parkway
Santa Clara, CA 95054
408-980-9770

REFERENCE

Periodicals

Aldus **magazine**
Aldus
411 First Avenue S.
Seattle, WA 98104
206-622-5500

Colophon
Font & Function
Adobe Systems, Inc.
PO Box 7900
Mountain View, CA 94039-7900
800-344-8335

MacUser
PC **magazine**
Ziff-Davis Publishing Company
1 Park Avenue
New York, NY 10016
800-627-2247

Macworld
IDG Communications
501 Second Street
San Francisco, CA 94107
800-234-1038

Personal Publishing
Hitchcock Publishing Company
191 S. Gary Avenue
Carol Stream, IL 60188
800-727-6937

Publish
PCW Communications
501 Second Street
San Francisco, CA 94107
800-222-2990

Step-by-Step Electronic Design
Dynamic Graphics
6000 N. Forest Park Drive
Peoria, IL 61614-3592
800-255-8800

U&lc
International Typeface
2 Hammarskjold Place
New York, NY 10017
212-371-0699

Verbum **magazine**
Verbum
PO Box 15439
San Diego, CA 92115
619-233-9977

Books

Desktop Publishing by Design
Microsoft Press
16011 N.E. 36th Way
Redmond, WA 98073-9717
206-882-8088

Expert Advisor: Adobe Illustrator
PostScript Language Reference Manual
Addison-Wesley Publishing
Jacob Way
Reading, MA 01867
215-779-5525

Looking Good in Print, Second Edition
The Makeover Book
Ventana Press
PO Box 2468
Chapel Hill, NC 27515
919-942-0220

Making Art on the Macintosh II
Scott, Foresman
1900 E. Lake Avenue
Glenview, IL 60025
708-729-3000

PostScript Type Sampler
MacTography
326D N. Stonestreet Avenue
Rockville, MD 20850
301-424-1357

Real World PageMaker 4
Bantam Books
666 Fifth Avenue
New York, NY 10103
800-223-6834

The Verbum Book of Postscript Illustration
The Verbum Book of Electronic Page Design
The Verbum Book of Digital Painting
The Verbum Book of Scanned Imagery
Verbum
PO Box 15439
San Diego, CA 92115
619-233-9977

Bulletin Board Services

CompuServe Information Services
5000 Arlington Center Boulevard
Columbus, OH 43260
800-848-8199

Connect Professional
Information Network
Connect
10161 Bubb Road
Cupertino, CA 95014
408-973-0110

Desktop Express
Dow Jones & Company
Princeton, NJ 08543
609-520-4000

Genie
GE Information Services
401 N. Washington Street
Rockville, MD 20850
800-638-9636

MCI Mail
MCI Mail
1150 17th Street N.W., Suite 800
Washington, DC 20036
800-444-6245

Index

T

U

the
Ventana Press

Desktop Design Series

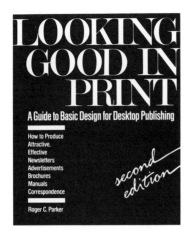

Inside Xerox Ventura Publisher: The Complete Learning and Reference Guide, Third Edition
$24.95
692 pages, Illustrated
ISBN: 0-940087-61-8

The all-time best-selling Ventura book is now revised and updated to give desktop publishers access to the full power of Ventura 3.0 and help them produce better-looking documents with strategies the pros use.

Newsletters from the Desktop
$23.95
290 pages, Illustrated
ISBN: 0-940087-40-5

Now the millions of desktop publishers who produce newsletters can learn how to improve the design of their publications.

The Makeover Book: 101 Design Solutions for Desktop Publishing
$17.95
245 pages, Illustrated
ISBN: 0-940087-20-0

"Before-and-after" desktop publishing examples demonstrate how basic design revisions can dramatically improve a document.

Type from the Desktop
$23.95
290 pages, Illustrated
ISBN: 0-940087-45-6

Learn the basics of designing with type from a desktop publisher's perspective.

Looking Good in Print, Second Edition
$23.95
410 pages, Illustrated
ISBN: 0-940087-32-4

With over 100,000 in print, **Looking Good in Print** is looking even better. More makeovers, a new section on designing newsletters and a wealth of new design tips and techniques to broaden the design skills of the ever-growing number of desktop publishers.

The Presentation Design Book
$24.95
280 pages, Illustrated
ISBN: 0-940087-37-5

How to design effective, attractive slides, overheads, graphs, diagrams, handouts and screen shows with your desktop computer.

Desktop Publishing with WordPerfect, Second Edition (For 5.0 and 5.1)
$21.95
350 pages, Illustrated
ISBN: 0-940087-47-2

WordPerfect offers graphics capabilities that can save users thousands of dollars in design and typesetting costs. Includes invaluable information on creating style sheets for consistency and speed.

TO ORDER additional copies of *The Gray Book* or any of the other books in our desktop design series, please fill out this order form and return it to us for quick shipment.

	Quantity		Price		Total
The Gray Book	_____	×	$22.95	=	$ _____
Looking Good in Print	_____	×	$23.95	=	$ _____
Desktop Publishing w/ WordPerfect	_____	×	$21.95	=	$ _____
Type from the Desktop	_____	×	$23.95	=	$ _____
The Presentation Design Book	_____	×	$24.95	=	$ _____
Newsletters from the Desktop	_____	×	$23.95	=	$ _____
The Makeover Book	_____	×	$17.95	=	$ _____
Inside Xerox Ventura Publisher	_____	×	$24.95	=	$ _____

Shipping: Please add $3.60/first book for standard UPS, $1.35/book thereafter; $6/book UPS "two-day air," $1.35/book thereafter. For Canada, add $5.35/book.   = $ _____

Send C.O.D. (add $3.30 to shipping charges)   = $ _____

North Carolina residents add 5% sales tax   = $ _____

Total   = $ _____

Name _____

Company _____

Address (No P.O. Box)_____

City _____ State _____ Zip _____

Daytime Phone _____

_____ Payment enclosed (check or money order; no cash please)

_____VISA   _____ MC   Acc't # _____ - _____ - _____ - _____

Expiration date _____   Signature_____

Please mail or fax to:

Ventana Press, P.O. Box 2468, Chapel Hill, NC 27515

919/942-0220, FAX: 919/942-1140.

TO ORDER additional copies of *The Gray Book* or any of the other books in our desktop design series, please fill out this order form and return it to us for quick shipment.

	Quantity		Price		Total
The Gray Book	_____	×	$22.95	=	$ _____
Looking Good in Print	_____	×	$23.95	=	$ _____
Desktop Publishing w/ WordPerfect	_____	×	$21.95	=	$ _____
Type from the Desktop	_____	×	$23.95	=	$ _____
The Presentation Design Book	_____	×	$24.95	=	$ _____
Newsletters from the Desktop	_____	×	$23.95	=	$ _____
The Makeover Book	_____	×	$17.95	=	$ _____
Inside Xerox Ventura Publisher	_____	×	$24.95	=	$ _____

Shipping: Please add $3.60/first book for standard UPS, $1.35/book thereafter; $6/book UPS "two-day air," $1.35/book thereafter. For Canada, add $5.35/book.   = $ _____

Send C.O.D. (add $3.30 to shipping charges)   = $ _____

North Carolina residents add 5% sales tax   = $ _____

Total   = $ _____

Name _____

Company _____

Address (No P.O. Box)_____

City _____ State _____ Zip _____

Daytime Phone _____

_____ Payment enclosed (check or money order; no cash please)

_____VISA   _____ MC   Acc't # _____ - _____ - _____ - _____

Expiration date _____ Signature_____

Please mail or fax to:

Ventana Press, P.O. Box 2468, Chapel Hill, NC 27515

919/942-0220, FAX: 919/942-1140.